C-3819 CAREER EXAMINATION SERIES

*This is your
PASSBOOK for...*

Swimming Pool Operator

*Test Preparation Study Guide
Questions & Answers*

COPYRIGHT NOTICE

This book is SOLELY intended for, is sold ONLY to, and its use is RESTRICTED to individual, bona fide applicants or candidates who qualify by virtue of having seriously filed applications for appropriate license, certificate, professional and/or promotional advancement, higher school matriculation, scholarship, or other legitimate requirements of education and/or governmental authorities.

This book is NOT intended for use, class instruction, tutoring, training, duplication, copying, reprinting, excerption, or adaptation, etc., by:

1) Other publishers
2) Proprietors and/or Instructors of "Coaching" and/or Preparatory Courses
3) Personnel and/or Training Divisions of commercial, industrial, and governmental organizations
4) Schools, colleges, or universities and/or their departments and staffs, including teachers and other personnel
5) Testing Agencies or Bureaus
6) Study groups which seek by the purchase of a single volume to copy and/or duplicate and/or adapt this material for use by the group as a whole without having purchased individual volumes for each of the members of the group
7) Et al.

Such persons would be in violation of appropriate Federal and State statutes.

PROVISION OF LICENSING AGREEMENTS – Recognized educational, commercial, industrial, and governmental institutions and organizations, and others legitimately engaged in educational pursuits, including training, testing, and measurement activities, may address request for a licensing agreement to the copyright owners, who will determine whether, and under what conditions, including fees and charges, the materials in this book may be used them. In other words, a licensing facility exists for the legitimate use of the material in this book on other than an individual basis. However, it is asseverated and affirmed here that the material in this book CANNOT be used without the receipt of the express permission of such a licensing agreement from the Publishers. Inquiries re licensing should be addressed to the company, attention rights and permissions department.

All rights reserved, including the right of reproduction in whole or in part, in any form or by any means, electronic or mechanical, including photocopying, recording, or by any information storage and retrieval system, without permission in writing from the Publisher.

Copyright © 2024 by
National Learning Corporation

212 Michael Drive, Syosset, NY 11791
(516) 921-8888 • www.passbooks.com
E-mail: info@passbooks.com

PASSBOOK® SERIES

THE *PASSBOOK® SERIES* has been created to prepare applicants and candidates for the ultimate academic battlefield – the examination room.

At some time in our lives, each and every one of us may be required to take an examination – for validation, matriculation, admission, qualification, registration, certification, or licensure.

Based on the assumption that every applicant or candidate has met the basic formal educational standards, has taken the required number of courses, and read the necessary texts, the *PASSBOOK® SERIES* furnishes the one special preparation which may assure passing with confidence, instead of failing with insecurity. Examination questions – together with answers – are furnished as the basic vehicle for study so that the mysteries of the examination and its compounding difficulties may be eliminated or diminished by a sure method.

This book is meant to help you pass your examination provided that you qualify and are serious in your objective.

The entire field is reviewed through the huge store of content information which is succinctly presented through a provocative and challenging approach – the question-and-answer method.

A climate of success is established by furnishing the correct answers at the end of each test.

You soon learn to recognize types of questions, forms of questions, and patterns of questioning. You may even begin to anticipate expected outcomes.

You perceive that many questions are repeated or adapted so that you can gain acute insights, which may enable you to score many sure points.

You learn how to confront new questions, or types of questions, and to attack them confidently and work out the correct answers.

You note objectives and emphases, and recognize pitfalls and dangers, so that you may make positive educational adjustments.

Moreover, you are kept fully informed in relation to new concepts, methods, practices, and directions in the field.

You discover that you are actually taking the examination all the time: you are preparing for the examination by "taking" an examination, not by reading extraneous and/or supererogatory textbooks.

In short, this PASSBOOK®, used directedly, should be an important factor in helping you to pass your test.

SWIMMING POOL OPERATOR

DUTIES
Under direct supervision, is responsible for the safe operation and maintenance of a swimming pool and adjacent areas in a school or park building; performs related duties as required. This position covers the construction, service, and repair of swimming pools and includes: excavation and grading; construction of concrete, gunite, and plastic-type pools, pool decks, and walkways, tiling and coping; and installation of equipment including pumps, filters, and chemical feeders.

SCOPE OF THE EXAMINATION
The multiple-choice written test will cover knowledge, skills, and/or abilities in such areas as:
1. Tools and their use;
2. Operation and maintenance of swimming pools and related facilities and equipment including: filtration/circulation systems, maintenance and operation, accessories and associated trades, concrete, shotcrete and gunite; erosion and sedimentation control; and
3. Cleanliness and safety in swimming pool areas.

HOW TO TAKE A TEST

I. YOU MUST PASS AN EXAMINATION

A. *WHAT EVERY CANDIDATE SHOULD KNOW*

Examination applicants often ask us for help in preparing for the written test. What can I study in advance? What kinds of questions will be asked? How will the test be given? How will the papers be graded?

As an applicant for a civil service examination, you may be wondering about some of these things. Our purpose here is to suggest effective methods of advance study and to describe civil service examinations.

Your chances for success on this examination can be increased if you know how to prepare. Those "pre-examination jitters" can be reduced if you know what to expect. You can even experience an adventure in good citizenship if you know why civil service exams are given.

B. *WHY ARE CIVIL SERVICE EXAMINATIONS GIVEN?*

Civil service examinations are important to you in two ways. As a citizen, you want public jobs filled by employees who know how to do their work. As a job seeker, you want a fair chance to compete for that job on an equal footing with other candidates. The best-known means of accomplishing this two-fold goal is the competitive examination.

Exams are widely publicized throughout the nation. They may be administered for jobs in federal, state, city, municipal, town or village governments or agencies.

Any citizen may apply, with some limitations, such as the age or residence of applicants. Your experience and education may be reviewed to see whether you meet the requirements for the particular examination. When these requirements exist, they are reasonable and applied consistently to all applicants. Thus, a competitive examination may cause you some uneasiness now, but it is your privilege and safeguard.

C. *HOW ARE CIVIL SERVICE EXAMS DEVELOPED?*

Examinations are carefully written by trained technicians who are specialists in the field known as "psychological measurement," in consultation with recognized authorities in the field of work that the test will cover. These experts recommend the subject matter areas or skills to be tested; only those knowledges or skills important to your success on the job are included. The most reliable books and source materials available are used as references. Together, the experts and technicians judge the difficulty level of the questions.

Test technicians know how to phrase questions so that the problem is clearly stated. Their ethics do not permit "trick" or "catch" questions. Questions may have been tried out on sample groups, or subjected to statistical analysis, to determine their usefulness.

Written tests are often used in combination with performance tests, ratings of training and experience, and oral interviews. All of these measures combine to form the best-known means of finding the right person for the right job.

II. HOW TO PASS THE WRITTEN TEST

A. NATURE OF THE EXAMINATION

To prepare intelligently for civil service examinations, you should know how they differ from school examinations you have taken. In school you were assigned certain definite pages to read or subjects to cover. The examination questions were quite detailed and usually emphasized memory. Civil service exams, on the other hand, try to discover your present ability to perform the duties of a position, plus your potentiality to learn these duties. In other words, a civil service exam attempts to predict how successful you will be. Questions cover such a broad area that they cannot be as minute and detailed as school exam questions.

In the public service similar kinds of work, or positions, are grouped together in one "class." This process is known as *position-classification*. All the positions in a class are paid according to the salary range for that class. One class title covers all of these positions, and they are all tested by the same examination.

B. FOUR BASIC STEPS

1) Study the announcement

How, then, can you know what subjects to study? Our best answer is: "Learn as much as possible about the class of positions for which you've applied." The exam will test the knowledge, skills and abilities needed to do the work.

Your most valuable source of information about the position you want is the official exam announcement. This announcement lists the training and experience qualifications. Check these standards and apply only if you come reasonably close to meeting them.

The brief description of the position in the examination announcement offers some clues to the subjects which will be tested. Think about the job itself. Review the duties in your mind. Can you perform them, or are there some in which you are rusty? Fill in the blank spots in your preparation.

Many jurisdictions preview the written test in the exam announcement by including a section called "Knowledge and Abilities Required," "Scope of the Examination," or some similar heading. Here you will find out specifically what fields will be tested.

2) Review your own background

Once you learn in general what the position is all about, and what you need to know to do the work, ask yourself which subjects you already know fairly well and which need improvement. You may wonder whether to concentrate on improving your strong areas or on building some background in your fields of weakness. When the announcement has specified "some knowledge" or "considerable knowledge," or has used adjectives like "beginning principles of…" or "advanced … methods," you can get a clue as to the number and difficulty of questions to be asked in any given field. More questions, and hence broader coverage, would be included for those subjects which are more important in the work. Now weigh your strengths and weaknesses against the job requirements and prepare accordingly.

3) Determine the level of the position

Another way to tell how intensively you should prepare is to understand the level of the job for which you are applying. Is it the entering level? In other words, is this the position in which beginners in a field of work are hired? Or is it an intermediate or advanced level? Sometimes this is indicated by such words as "Junior" or "Senior" in the class title. Other jurisdictions use Roman numerals to designate the level – Clerk I, Clerk II, for example. The word "Supervisor" sometimes appears in the title. If the level is not indicated by the title, check the description of duties. Will you be working under very close supervision, or will you have responsibility for independent decisions in this work?

4) Choose appropriate study materials

Now that you know the subjects to be examined and the relative amount of each subject to be covered, you can choose suitable study materials. For beginning level jobs, or even advanced ones, if you have a pronounced weakness in some aspect of your training, read a modern, standard textbook in that field. Be sure it is up to date and has general coverage. Such books are normally available at your library, and the librarian will be glad to help you locate one. For entry-level positions, questions of appropriate difficulty are chosen – neither highly advanced questions, nor those too simple. Such questions require careful thought but not advanced training.

If the position for which you are applying is technical or advanced, you will read more advanced, specialized material. If you are already familiar with the basic principles of your field, elementary textbooks would waste your time. Concentrate on advanced textbooks and technical periodicals. Think through the concepts and review difficult problems in your field.

These are all general sources. You can get more ideas on your own initiative, following these leads. For example, training manuals and publications of the government agency which employs workers in your field can be useful, particularly for technical and professional positions. A letter or visit to the government department involved may result in more specific study suggestions, and certainly will provide you with a more definite idea of the exact nature of the position you are seeking.

III. KINDS OF TESTS

Tests are used for purposes other than measuring knowledge and ability to perform specified duties. For some positions, it is equally important to test ability to make adjustments to new situations or to profit from training. In others, basic mental abilities not dependent on information are essential. Questions which test these things may not appear as pertinent to the duties of the position as those which test for knowledge and information. Yet they are often highly important parts of a fair examination. For very general questions, it is almost impossible to help you direct your study efforts. What we can do is to point out some of the more common of these general abilities needed in public service positions and describe some typical questions.

1) General information

Broad, general information has been found useful for predicting job success in some kinds of work. This is tested in a variety of ways, from vocabulary lists to questions about current events. Basic background in some field of work, such as sociology or economics, may be sampled in a group of questions. Often these are principles which have become familiar to most persons through exposure rather than through formal training. It is difficult to advise you how to study for these questions; being alert to the world around you is our best suggestion.

2) Verbal ability

An example of an ability needed in many positions is verbal or language ability. Verbal ability is, in brief, the ability to use and understand words. Vocabulary and grammar tests are typical measures of this ability. Reading comprehension or paragraph interpretation questions are common in many kinds of civil service tests. You are given a paragraph of written material and asked to find its central meaning.

3) Numerical ability
Number skills can be tested by the familiar arithmetic problem, by checking paired lists of numbers to see which are alike and which are different, or by interpreting charts and graphs. In the latter test, a graph may be printed in the test booklet which you are asked to use as the basis for answering questions.

4) Observation
A popular test for law-enforcement positions is the observation test. A picture is shown to you for several minutes, then taken away. Questions about the picture test your ability to observe both details and larger elements.

5) Following directions
In many positions in the public service, the employee must be able to carry out written instructions dependably and accurately. You may be given a chart with several columns, each column listing a variety of information. The questions require you to carry out directions involving the information given in the chart.

6) Skills and aptitudes
Performance tests effectively measure some manual skills and aptitudes. When the skill is one in which you are trained, such as typing or shorthand, you can practice. These tests are often very much like those given in business school or high school courses. For many of the other skills and aptitudes, however, no short-time preparation can be made. Skills and abilities natural to you or that you have developed throughout your lifetime are being tested.

Many of the general questions just described provide all the data needed to answer the questions and ask you to use your reasoning ability to find the answers. Your best preparation for these tests, as well as for tests of facts and ideas, is to be at your physical and mental best. You, no doubt, have your own methods of getting into an exam-taking mood and keeping "in shape." The next section lists some ideas on this subject.

IV. KINDS OF QUESTIONS

Only rarely is the "essay" question, which you answer in narrative form, used in civil service tests. Civil service tests are usually of the short-answer type. Full instructions for answering these questions will be given to you at the examination. But in case this is your first experience with short-answer questions and separate answer sheets, here is what you need to know:

1) Multiple-choice Questions

Most popular of the short-answer questions is the "multiple choice" or "best answer" question. It can be used, for example, to test for factual knowledge, ability to solve problems or judgment in meeting situations found at work.

A multiple-choice question is normally one of three types—
- It can begin with an incomplete statement followed by several possible endings. You are to find the one ending which *best* completes the statement, although some of the others may not be entirely wrong.
- It can also be a complete statement in the form of a question which is answered by choosing one of the statements listed.

- It can be in the form of a problem – again you select the best answer.

Here is an example of a multiple-choice question with a discussion which should give you some clues as to the method for choosing the right answer:

When an employee has a complaint about his assignment, the action which will *best* help him overcome his difficulty is to
   A. discuss his difficulty with his coworkers
   B. take the problem to the head of the organization
   C. take the problem to the person who gave him the assignment
   D. say nothing to anyone about his complaint

In answering this question, you should study each of the choices to find which is best. Consider choice "A" – Certainly an employee may discuss his complaint with fellow employees, but no change or improvement can result, and the complaint remains unresolved. Choice "B" is a poor choice since the head of the organization probably does not know what assignment you have been given, and taking your problem to him is known as "going over the head" of the supervisor. The supervisor, or person who made the assignment, is the person who can clarify it or correct any injustice. Choice "C" is, therefore, correct. To say nothing, as in choice "D," is unwise. Supervisors have and interest in knowing the problems employees are facing, and the employee is seeking a solution to his problem.

2) True/False Questions

The "true/false" or "right/wrong" form of question is sometimes used. Here a complete statement is given. Your job is to decide whether the statement is right or wrong.

SAMPLE: A roaming cell-phone call to a nearby city costs less than a non-roaming call to a distant city.

This statement is wrong, or false, since roaming calls are more expensive.

This is not a complete list of all possible question forms, although most of the others are variations of these common types. You will always get complete directions for answering questions. Be sure you understand *how* to mark your answers – ask questions until you do.

V. RECORDING YOUR ANSWERS

Computer terminals are used more and more today for many different kinds of exams.
For an examination with very few applicants, you may be told to record your answers in the test booklet itself. Separate answer sheets are much more common. If this separate answer sheet is to be scored by machine – and this is often the case – it is highly important that you mark your answers correctly in order to get credit.
An electronic scoring machine is often used in civil service offices because of the speed with which papers can be scored. Machine-scored answer sheets must be marked with a pencil, which will be given to you. This pencil has a high graphite content which responds to the electronic scoring machine. As a matter of fact, stray dots may register as answers, so do not let your pencil rest on the answer sheet while you are pondering the correct answer. Also, if your pencil lead breaks or is otherwise defective, ask for another.

Since the answer sheet will be dropped in a slot in the scoring machine, be careful not to bend the corners or get the paper crumpled.

The answer sheet normally has five vertical columns of numbers, with 30 numbers to a column. These numbers correspond to the question numbers in your test booklet. After each number, going across the page are four or five pairs of dotted lines. These short dotted lines have small letters or numbers above them. The first two pairs may also have a "T" or "F" above the letters. This indicates that the first two pairs only are to be used if the questions are of the true-false type. If the questions are multiple choice, disregard the "T" and "F" and pay attention only to the small letters or numbers.

Answer your questions in the manner of the sample that follows:

32. The largest city in the United States is
    A. Washington, D.C.
    B. New York City
    C. Chicago
    D. Detroit
    E. San Francisco

1) Choose the answer you think is best. (New York City is the largest, so "B" is correct.)
2) Find the row of dotted lines numbered the same as the question you are answering. (Find row number 32)
3) Find the pair of dotted lines corresponding to the answer. (Find the pair of lines under the mark "B.")
4) Make a solid black mark between the dotted lines.

VI. BEFORE THE TEST

Common sense will help you find procedures to follow to get ready for an examination. Too many of us, however, overlook these sensible measures. Indeed, nervousness and fatigue have been found to be the most serious reasons why applicants fail to do their best on civil service tests. Here is a list of reminders:

- Begin your preparation early – Don't wait until the last minute to go scurrying around for books and materials or to find out what the position is all about.
- Prepare continuously – An hour a night for a week is better than an all-night cram session. This has been definitely established. What is more, a night a week for a month will return better dividends than crowding your study into a shorter period of time.
- Locate the place of the exam – You have been sent a notice telling you when and where to report for the examination. If the location is in a different town or otherwise unfamiliar to you, it would be well to inquire the best route and learn something about the building.
- Relax the night before the test – Allow your mind to rest. Do not study at all that night. Plan some mild recreation or diversion; then go to bed early and get a good night's sleep.
- Get up early enough to make a leisurely trip to the place for the test – This way unforeseen events, traffic snarls, unfamiliar buildings, etc. will not upset you.
- Dress comfortably – A written test is not a fashion show. You will be known by number and not by name, so wear something comfortable.

- Leave excess paraphernalia at home – Shopping bags and odd bundles will get in your way. You need bring only the items mentioned in the official notice you received; usually everything you need is provided. Do not bring reference books to the exam. They will only confuse those last minutes and be taken away from you when in the test room.
- Arrive somewhat ahead of time – If because of transportation schedules you must get there very early, bring a newspaper or magazine to take your mind off yourself while waiting.
- Locate the examination room – When you have found the proper room, you will be directed to the seat or part of the room where you will sit. Sometimes you are given a sheet of instructions to read while you are waiting. Do not fill out any forms until you are told to do so; just read them and be prepared.
- Relax and prepare to listen to the instructions
- If you have any physical problem that may keep you from doing your best, be sure to tell the test administrator. If you are sick or in poor health, you really cannot do your best on the exam. You can come back and take the test some other time.

VII. AT THE TEST

The day of the test is here and you have the test booklet in your hand. The temptation to get going is very strong. Caution! There is more to success than knowing the right answers. You must know how to identify your papers and understand variations in the type of short-answer question used in this particular examination. Follow these suggestions for maximum results from your efforts:

1) Cooperate with the monitor
The test administrator has a duty to create a situation in which you can be as much at ease as possible. He will give instructions, tell you when to begin, check to see that you are marking your answer sheet correctly, and so on. He is not there to guard you, although he will see that your competitors do not take unfair advantage. He wants to help you do your best.

2) Listen to all instructions
Don't jump the gun! Wait until you understand all directions. In most civil service tests you get more time than you need to answer the questions. So don't be in a hurry. Read each word of instructions until you clearly understand the meaning. Study the examples, listen to all announcements and follow directions. Ask questions if you do not understand what to do.

3) Identify your papers
Civil service exams are usually identified by number only. You will be assigned a number; you must not put your name on your test papers. Be sure to copy your number correctly. Since more than one exam may be given, copy your exact examination title.

4) Plan your time
Unless you are told that a test is a "speed" or "rate of work" test, speed itself is usually not important. Time enough to answer all the questions will be provided, but this does not mean that you have all day. An overall time limit has been set. Divide the total time (in minutes) by the number of questions to determine the approximate time you have for each question.

5) Do not linger over difficult questions

If you come across a difficult question, mark it with a paper clip (useful to have along) and come back to it when you have been through the booklet. One caution if you do this – be sure to skip a number on your answer sheet as well. Check often to be sure that you have not lost your place and that you are marking in the row numbered the same as the question you are answering.

6) Read the questions

Be sure you know what the question asks! Many capable people are unsuccessful because they failed to *read* the questions correctly.

7) Answer all questions

Unless you have been instructed that a penalty will be deducted for incorrect answers, it is better to guess than to omit a question.

8) Speed tests

It is often better NOT to guess on speed tests. It has been found that on timed tests people are tempted to spend the last few seconds before time is called in marking answers at random – without even reading them – in the hope of picking up a few extra points. To discourage this practice, the instructions may warn you that your score will be "corrected" for guessing. That is, a penalty will be applied. The incorrect answers will be deducted from the correct ones, or some other penalty formula will be used.

9) Review your answers

If you finish before time is called, go back to the questions you guessed or omitted to give them further thought. Review other answers if you have time.

10) Return your test materials

If you are ready to leave before others have finished or time is called, take ALL your materials to the monitor and leave quietly. Never take any test material with you. The monitor can discover whose papers are not complete, and taking a test booklet may be grounds for disqualification.

VIII. EXAMINATION TECHNIQUES

1) Read the general instructions carefully. These are usually printed on the first page of the exam booklet. As a rule, these instructions refer to the timing of the examination; the fact that you should not start work until the signal and must stop work at a signal, etc. If there are any *special* instructions, such as a choice of questions to be answered, make sure that you note this instruction carefully.

2) When you are ready to start work on the examination, that is as soon as the signal has been given, read the instructions to each question booklet, underline any key words or phrases, such as *least, best, outline, describe* and the like. In this way you will tend to answer as requested rather than discover on reviewing your paper that you *listed without describing*, that you selected the *worst* choice rather than the *best* choice, etc.

3) If the examination is of the objective or multiple-choice type – that is, each question will also give a series of possible answers: A, B, C or D, and you are called upon to select the best answer and write the letter next to that answer on your answer paper – it is advisable to start answering each question in turn. There may be anywhere from 50 to 100 such questions in the three or four hours allotted and you can see how much time would be taken if you read through all the questions before beginning to answer any. Furthermore, if you come across a question or group of questions which you know would be difficult to answer, it would undoubtedly affect your handling of all the other questions.

4) If the examination is of the essay type and contains but a few questions, it is a moot point as to whether you should read all the questions before starting to answer any one. Of course, if you are given a choice – say five out of seven and the like – then it is essential to read all the questions so you can eliminate the two that are most difficult. If, however, you are asked to answer all the questions, there may be danger in trying to answer the easiest one first because you may find that you will spend too much time on it. The best technique is to answer the first question, then proceed to the second, etc.

5) Time your answers. Before the exam begins, write down the time it started, then add the time allowed for the examination and write down the time it must be completed, then divide the time available somewhat as follows:
   - If 3-1/2 hours are allowed, that would be 210 minutes. If you have 80 objective-type questions, that would be an average of 2-1/2 minutes per question. Allow yourself no more than 2 minutes per question, or a total of 160 minutes, which will permit about 50 minutes to review.
   - If for the time allotment of 210 minutes there are 7 essay questions to answer, that would average about 30 minutes a question. Give yourself only 25 minutes per question so that you have about 35 minutes to review.

6) The most important instruction is to *read each question* and make sure you know what is wanted. The second most important instruction is to *time yourself properly* so that you answer every question. The third most important instruction is to *answer every question*. Guess if you have to but include something for each question. Remember that you will receive no credit for a blank and will probably receive some credit if you write something in answer to an essay question. If you guess a letter – say "B" for a multiple-choice question – you may have guessed right. If you leave a blank as an answer to a multiple-choice question, the examiners may respect your feelings but it will not add a point to your score. Some exams may penalize you for wrong answers, so in such cases *only*, you may not want to guess unless you have some basis for your answer.

7) Suggestions
   a. Objective-type questions
      1. Examine the question booklet for proper sequence of pages and questions
      2. Read all instructions carefully
      3. Skip any question which seems too difficult; return to it after all other questions have been answered
      4. Apportion your time properly; do not spend too much time on any single question or group of questions

5. Note and underline key words – *all, most, fewest, least, best, worst, same, opposite*, etc.
6. Pay particular attention to negatives
7. Note unusual option, e.g., unduly long, short, complex, different or similar in content to the body of the question
8. Observe the use of "hedging" words – *probably, may, most likely*, etc.
9. Make sure that your answer is put next to the same number as the question
10. Do not second-guess unless you have good reason to believe the second answer is definitely more correct
11. Cross out original answer if you decide another answer is more accurate; do not erase until you are ready to hand your paper in
12. Answer all questions; guess unless instructed otherwise
13. Leave time for review

  b. Essay questions
   1. Read each question carefully
   2. Determine exactly what is wanted. Underline key words or phrases.
   3. Decide on outline or paragraph answer
   4. Include many different points and elements unless asked to develop any one or two points or elements
   5. Show impartiality by giving pros and cons unless directed to select one side only
   6. Make and write down any assumptions you find necessary to answer the questions
   7. Watch your English, grammar, punctuation and choice of words
   8. Time your answers; don't crowd material

8) Answering the essay question

Most essay questions can be answered by framing the specific response around several key words or ideas. Here are a few such key words or ideas:

M's: manpower, materials, methods, money, management
P's: purpose, program, policy, plan, procedure, practice, problems, pitfalls, personnel, public relations
  a. Six basic steps in handling problems:
   1. Preliminary plan and background development
   2. Collect information, data and facts
   3. Analyze and interpret information, data and facts
   4. Analyze and develop solutions as well as make recommendations
   5. Prepare report and sell recommendations
   6. Install recommendations and follow up effectiveness

  b. Pitfalls to avoid
   1. *Taking things for granted* – A statement of the situation does not necessarily imply that each of the elements is necessarily true; for example, a complaint may be invalid and biased so that all that can be taken for granted is that a complaint has been registered

2. *Considering only one side of a situation* – Wherever possible, indicate several alternatives and then point out the reasons you selected the best one
3. *Failing to indicate follow up* – Whenever your answer indicates action on your part, make certain that you will take proper follow-up action to see how successful your recommendations, procedures or actions turn out to be
4. *Taking too long in answering any single question* – Remember to time your answers properly

IX. AFTER THE TEST

Scoring procedures differ in detail among civil service jurisdictions although the general principles are the same. Whether the papers are hand-scored or graded by machine we have described, they are nearly always graded by number. That is, the person who marks the paper knows only the number – never the name – of the applicant. Not until all the papers have been graded will they be matched with names. If other tests, such as training and experience or oral interview ratings have been given, scores will be combined. Different parts of the examination usually have different weights. For example, the written test might count 60 percent of the final grade, and a rating of training and experience 40 percent. In many jurisdictions, veterans will have a certain number of points added to their grades.

After the final grade has been determined, the names are placed in grade order and an eligible list is established. There are various methods for resolving ties between those who get the same final grade – probably the most common is to place first the name of the person whose application was received first. Job offers are made from the eligible list in the order the names appear on it. You will be notified of your grade and your rank as soon as all these computations have been made. This will be done as rapidly as possible.

People who are found to meet the requirements in the announcement are called "eligibles." Their names are put on a list of eligible candidates. An eligible's chances of getting a job depend on how high he stands on this list and how fast agencies are filling jobs from the list.

When a job is to be filled from a list of eligibles, the agency asks for the names of people on the list of eligibles for that job. When the civil service commission receives this request, it sends to the agency the names of the three people highest on this list. Or, if the job to be filled has specialized requirements, the office sends the agency the names of the top three persons who meet these requirements from the general list.

The appointing officer makes a choice from among the three people whose names were sent to him. If the selected person accepts the appointment, the names of the others are put back on the list to be considered for future openings.

That is the rule in hiring from all kinds of eligible lists, whether they are for typist, carpenter, chemist, or something else. For every vacancy, the appointing officer has his choice of any one of the top three eligibles on the list. This explains why the person whose name is on top of the list sometimes does not get an appointment when some of the persons lower on the list do. If the appointing officer chooses the second or third eligible, the No. 1 eligible does not get a job at once, but stays on the list until he is appointed or the list is terminated.

X. HOW TO PASS THE INTERVIEW TEST

The examination for which you applied requires an oral interview test. You have already taken the written test and you are now being called for the interview test – the final part of the formal examination.

You may think that it is not possible to prepare for an interview test and that there are no procedures to follow during an interview. Our purpose is to point out some things you can do in advance that will help you and some good rules to follow and pitfalls to avoid while you are being interviewed.

What is an interview supposed to test?

The written examination is designed to test the technical knowledge and competence of the candidate; the oral is designed to evaluate intangible qualities, not readily measured otherwise, and to establish a list showing the relative fitness of each candidate – as measured against his competitors – for the position sought. Scoring is not on the basis of "right" and "wrong," but on a sliding scale of values ranging from "not passable" to "outstanding." As a matter of fact, it is possible to achieve a relatively low score without a single "incorrect" answer because of evident weakness in the qualities being measured.

Occasionally, an examination may consist entirely of an oral test – either an individual or a group oral. In such cases, information is sought concerning the technical knowledges and abilities of the candidate, since there has been no written examination for this purpose. More commonly, however, an oral test is used to supplement a written examination.

Who conducts interviews?

The composition of oral boards varies among different jurisdictions. In nearly all, a representative of the personnel department serves as chairman. One of the members of the board may be a representative of the department in which the candidate would work. In some cases, "outside experts" are used, and, frequently, a businessman or some other representative of the general public is asked to serve. Labor and management or other special groups may be represented. The aim is to secure the services of experts in the appropriate field.

However the board is composed, it is a good idea (and not at all improper or unethical) to ascertain in advance of the interview who the members are and what groups they represent. When you are introduced to them, you will have some idea of their backgrounds and interests, and at least you will not stutter and stammer over their names.

What should be done before the interview?

While knowledge about the board members is useful and takes some of the surprise element out of the interview, there is other preparation which is more substantive. It *is* possible to prepare for an oral interview – in several ways:

1) Keep a copy of your application and review it carefully before the interview

This may be the only document before the oral board, and the starting point of the interview. Know what education and experience you have listed there, and the sequence and dates of all of it. Sometimes the board will ask you to review the highlights of your experience for them; you should not have to hem and haw doing it.

2) Study the class specification and the examination announcement

Usually, the oral board has one or both of these to guide them. The qualities, characteristics or knowledges required by the position sought are stated in these documents. They offer valuable clues as to the nature of the oral interview. For example, if the job involves supervisory responsibilities, the announcement will usually indicate that knowledge of modern supervisory methods and the qualifications of the candidate as a supervisor will be tested. If so, you can expect such questions, frequently in the form of a hypothetical situation which you are expected to solve. NEVER go into an oral without knowledge of the duties and responsibilities of the job you seek.

3) Think through each qualification required

Try to visualize the kind of questions you would ask if you were a board member. How well could you answer them? Try especially to appraise your own knowledge and background in each area, *measured against the job sought*, and identify any areas in which you are weak. Be critical and realistic – do not flatter yourself.

4) Do some general reading in areas in which you feel you may be weak

For example, if the job involves supervision and your past experience has NOT, some general reading in supervisory methods and practices, particularly in the field of human relations, might be useful. Do NOT study agency procedures or detailed manuals. The oral board will be testing your understanding and capacity, not your memory.

5) Get a good night's sleep and watch your general health and mental attitude

You will want a clear head at the interview. Take care of a cold or any other minor ailment, and of course, no hangovers.

What should be done on the day of the interview?

Now comes the day of the interview itself. Give yourself plenty of time to get there. Plan to arrive somewhat ahead of the scheduled time, particularly if your appointment is in the fore part of the day. If a previous candidate fails to appear, the board might be ready for you a bit early. By early afternoon an oral board is almost invariably behind schedule if there are many candidates, and you may have to wait. Take along a book or magazine to read, or your application to review, but leave any extraneous material in the waiting room when you go in for your interview. In any event, relax and compose yourself.

The matter of dress is important. The board is forming impressions about you – from your experience, your manners, your attitude, and your appearance. Give your personal appearance careful attention. Dress your best, but not your flashiest. Choose conservative, appropriate clothing, and be sure it is immaculate. This is a business interview, and your appearance should indicate that you regard it as such. Besides, being well groomed and properly dressed will help boost your confidence.

Sooner or later, someone will call your name and escort you into the interview room. *This is it.* From here on you are on your own. It is too late for any more preparation. But remember, you asked for this opportunity to prove your fitness, and you are here because your request was granted.

What happens when you go in?

The usual sequence of events will be as follows: The clerk (who is often the board stenographer) will introduce you to the chairman of the oral board, who will introduce you to the other members of the board. Acknowledge the introductions before you sit down. Do not be surprised if you find a microphone facing you or a stenotypist sitting by. Oral interviews are usually recorded in the event of an appeal or other review.

Usually the chairman of the board will open the interview by reviewing the highlights of your education and work experience from your application – primarily for the benefit of the other members of the board, as well as to get the material into the record. Do not interrupt or comment unless there is an error or significant misinterpretation; if that is the case, do not hesitate. But do not quibble about insignificant matters. Also, he will usually ask you some question about your education, experience or your present job – partly to get you to start talking and to establish the interviewing "rapport." He may start the actual questioning, or turn it over to one of the other members. Frequently, each member undertakes the questioning on a particular area, one in which he is perhaps most competent, so you can expect each member to participate in the examination. Because time is limited, you may also expect some rather abrupt switches in the direction the questioning takes, so do not be upset by it. Normally, a board member will not pursue a single line of questioning unless he discovers a particular strength or weakness.

After each member has participated, the chairman will usually ask whether any member has any further questions, then will ask you if you have anything you wish to add. Unless you are expecting this question, it may floor you. Worse, it may start you off on an extended, extemporaneous speech. The board is not usually seeking more information. The question is principally to offer you a last opportunity to present further qualifications or to indicate that you have nothing to add. So, if you feel that a significant qualification or characteristic has been overlooked, it is proper to point it out in a sentence or so. Do not compliment the board on the thoroughness of their examination – they have been sketchy, and you know it. If you wish, merely say, "No thank you, I have nothing further to add." This is a point where you can "talk yourself out" of a good impression or fail to present an important bit of information. Remember, *you close the interview yourself.*

The chairman will then say, "That is all, Mr. _____, thank you." Do not be startled; the interview is over, and quicker than you think. Thank him, gather your belongings and take your leave. Save your sigh of relief for the other side of the door.

How to put your best foot forward

Throughout this entire process, you may feel that the board individually and collectively is trying to pierce your defenses, seek out your hidden weaknesses and embarrass and confuse you. Actually, this is not true. They are obliged to make an appraisal of your qualifications for the job you are seeking, and they want to see you in your best light. Remember, they must interview all candidates and a non-cooperative candidate may become a failure in spite of their best efforts to bring out his qualifications. Here are 15 suggestions that will help you:

1) Be natural – Keep your attitude confident, not cocky

If you are not confident that you can do the job, do not expect the board to be. Do not apologize for your weaknesses, try to bring out your strong points. The board is interested in a positive, not negative, presentation. Cockiness will antagonize any board member and make him wonder if you are covering up a weakness by a false show of strength.

2) Get comfortable, but don't lounge or sprawl

Sit erectly but not stiffly. A careless posture may lead the board to conclude that you are careless in other things, or at least that you are not impressed by the importance of the occasion. Either conclusion is natural, even if incorrect. Do not fuss with your clothing, a pencil or an ashtray. Your hands may occasionally be useful to emphasize a point; do not let them become a point of distraction.

3) Do not wisecrack or make small talk

This is a serious situation, and your attitude should show that you consider it as such. Further, the time of the board is limited – they do not want to waste it, and neither should you.

4) Do not exaggerate your experience or abilities
In the first place, from information in the application or other interviews and sources, the board may know more about you than you think. Secondly, you probably will not get away with it. An experienced board is rather adept at spotting such a situation, so do not take the chance.

5) If you know a board member, do not make a point of it, yet do not hide it
Certainly you are not fooling him, and probably not the other members of the board. Do not try to take advantage of your acquaintanceship – it will probably do you little good.

6) Do not dominate the interview
Let the board do that. They will give you the clues – do not assume that you have to do all the talking. Realize that the board has a number of questions to ask you, and do not try to take up all the interview time by showing off your extensive knowledge of the answer to the first one.

7) Be attentive
You only have 20 minutes or so, and you should keep your attention at its sharpest throughout. When a member is addressing a problem or question to you, give him your undivided attention. Address your reply principally to him, but do not exclude the other board members.

8) Do not interrupt
A board member may be stating a problem for you to analyze. He will ask you a question when the time comes. Let him state the problem, and wait for the question.

9) Make sure you understand the question
Do not try to answer until you are sure what the question is. If it is not clear, restate it in your own words or ask the board member to clarify it for you. However, do not haggle about minor elements.

10) Reply promptly but not hastily
A common entry on oral board rating sheets is "candidate responded readily," or "candidate hesitated in replies." Respond as promptly and quickly as you can, but do not jump to a hasty, ill-considered answer.

11) Do not be peremptory in your answers
A brief answer is proper – but do not fire your answer back. That is a losing game from your point of view. The board member can probably ask questions much faster than you can answer them.

12) Do not try to create the answer you think the board member wants
He is interested in what kind of mind you have and how it works – not in playing games. Furthermore, he can usually spot this practice and will actually grade you down on it.

13) Do not switch sides in your reply merely to agree with a board member
Frequently, a member will take a contrary position merely to draw you out and to see if you are willing and able to defend your point of view. Do not start a debate, yet do not surrender a good position. If a position is worth taking, it is worth defending.

14) Do not be afraid to admit an error in judgment if you are shown to be wrong

The board knows that you are forced to reply without any opportunity for careful consideration. Your answer may be demonstrably wrong. If so, admit it and get on with the interview.

15) Do not dwell at length on your present job

The opening question may relate to your present assignment. Answer the question but do not go into an extended discussion. You are being examined for a *new* job, not your present one. As a matter of fact, try to phrase ALL your answers in terms of the job for which you are being examined.

Basis of Rating

Probably you will forget most of these "do's" and "don'ts" when you walk into the oral interview room. Even remembering them all will not ensure you a passing grade. Perhaps you did not have the qualifications in the first place. But remembering them will help you to put your best foot forward, without treading on the toes of the board members.

Rumor and popular opinion to the contrary notwithstanding, an oral board wants you to make the best appearance possible. They know you are under pressure – but they also want to see how you respond to it as a guide to what your reaction would be under the pressures of the job you seek. They will be influenced by the degree of poise you display, the personal traits you show and the manner in which you respond.

ABOUT THIS BOOK

This book contains tests divided into Examination Sections. Go through each test, answering every question in the margin. We have also attached a sample answer sheet at the back of the book that can be removed and used. At the end of each test look at the answer key and check your answers. On the ones you got wrong, look at the right answer choice and learn. Do not fill in the answers first. Do not memorize the questions and answers, but understand the answer and principles involved. On your test, the questions will likely be different from the samples. Questions are changed and new ones added. If you understand these past questions you should have success with any changes that arise. Tests may consist of several types of questions. We have additional books on each subject should more study be advisable or necessary for you. Finally, the more you study, the better prepared you will be. This book is intended to be the last thing you study before you walk into the examination room. Prior study of relevant texts is also recommended. NLC publishes some of these in our Fundamental Series. Knowledge and good sense are important factors in passing your exam. Good luck also helps. So now study this Passbook, absorb the material contained within and take that knowledge into the examination. Then do your best to pass that exam.

EXAMINATION SECTION

EXAMINATION SECTION
TEST 1

DIRECTIONS: Each question or incomplete statement is followed by several suggested answers or completions. Select the one that BEST answers the question or completes the statement. *PRINT THE LETTER OF THE CORRECT ANSWER IN THE SPACE AT THE RIGHT.*

1. If the pH level in a pool is too high, the proper remedy is to

    A. add sodium bicarbonate
    B. superchlorinate the water
    C. thoroughly skim the pool
    D. add muriatic acid

2. If nildew or fungus is present on the concrete surface of a pool, it can be killed or removed by using a cleaner containing
    I. trisodium phosphate
    II. muriatic acid
    III. sodium hypochlorite
   The CORRECT answer is:

    A. I *only*   B. I, II   C. I, III   D. II, III

3. Though seldom used as a pool disinfectant, iodine has the advantage over chlorine of

    A. causing less eye irritation
    B. greater durability
    C. acting as a more effective algaecide
    D. not clouding or discoloring pool water

4. For a small pool (fewer than 18,000 gallon capacity), a filter pump with a _____ horsepower motor is usually sufficient.

    A. 1/4   B. 1/3   C. 1/2   D. 3/4

5. If a pool filter's water flow is restricted, which of the following should be tried FIRST?

    A. Check skimmer and pump strainer baskets for debris
    B. Check for algae in pool
    C. Check surface of filter sand bed
    D. Backwash the filter

6. What is the term for adding a chemical to pool water for the purpose of settling suspended dirt or other solids to the pool floor?

    A. Floccing   B. Copsing
    C. Feathering   D. Coagulation

7. Typically, pool alkalinity takes one or more of three forms. Which of the following is NOT one of these forms?

    A. Carbonate   B. Hydroxide
    C. Hypochlorite   D. Bicarbonate

8. The recommended chlorine residual for most swimming pools is _____ parts per million.

   A. 0.25 to 0.5
   B. 0.5 to 0.75
   C. 1.0 to 1.5
   D. 1.75 to 2.25

9. The pH blocks used to counteract acidity in pool water are typically fused cakes of

   A. ammonium crystals
   B. lye
   C. chloride
   D. soda ash

10. It is generally best to add chlorine to pool water

    A. in the morning
    B. around midday
    C. in the early evening
    D. at night

11. The piping which carries filtered water from the filter to the pool is referred to as _____ piping.

    A. recirculating
    B. return
    C. backwash
    D. face

12. Each of the following is a sign that the chlorine used to disinfect a pool is in a combined state EXCEPT

    A. grayish or cloudy pool water
    B. strong odor of chlorine
    C. swimmers complaining of eye irritation
    D. pH readings of 8.0 or above

13. The general rule for settling on a comfortable temperature for pool water is to begin at _____ °F and adjust either upward or downward from there, depending on comfort.

    A. 60   B. 70   C. 80   D. 90

14. If an automatic pool cleaner is used with a filter system, it is important that the return fitting be located

    A. within six inches in either direction of the filter unit
    B. at the center of the long wall opposite the filter system
    C. adjacent to the skimmer
    D. at the center of the long wall closest to the filter system

15. The MOST common method for testing chlorine residual in a swimming pool is the

    A. DPD test
    B. total alkalinity test
    C. orthotolidine color test
    D. simple test strip

16. When re-opening a pool after the winter, which of the following steps is typically performed LAST?

    A. Raising water level
    B. Establishing free chlorine residual
    C. Vacuuming pool
    D. Adding conditioner

17. As a rule of thumb, a pool's heater should be able to heat the water in the pool at a rate of _____ degree(s) per _____.   17____

    A. one; three hours
    B. one; hour
    C. two; hour
    D. five; hour

18. Which of the following types of paint would be MOST appropriate for use with concrete pools?   18____

    A. Oil-based glazing compound
    B. Solvent-thinned latex enamel
    C. Solvent-thinned oil-based enamel
    D. Unthinned catalyzed epoxy

19. For a medium-sized pool of an 18,000-30,000 gallon capacity, what diameter size of sand filter would be most appropriate?   19____

    A. 18-inch   B. 24-inch   C. 30-inch   D. 36-inch

Questions 20-25.

DIRECTIONS: Questions 20 through 25 refer to the figure below, a diagram of a typical sand pool filter. Place the letter that corresponds to each element in the space at the right.

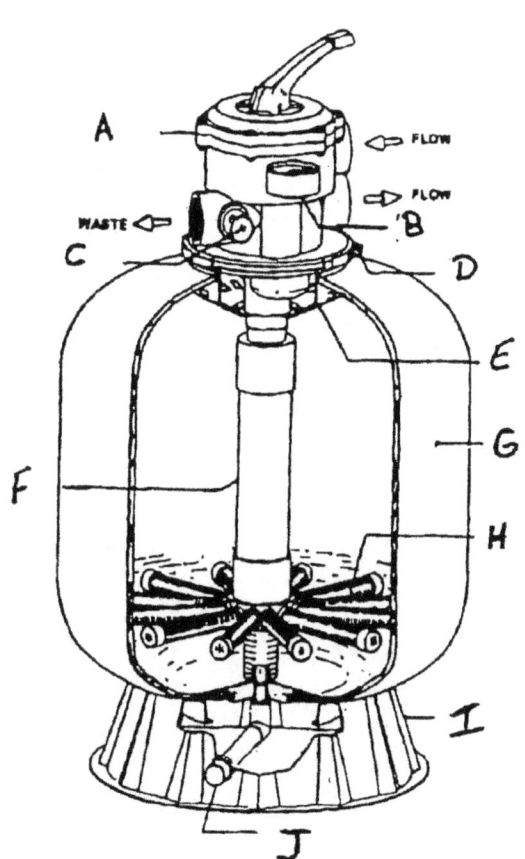

20. Sight glass 20____
21. Multi-port dial valve 21____
22. Slotted lateral filter assembly 22____
23. Backwash indicator 23____
24. Tank drain 24____
25. Inlet water distributor 25____

KEY (CORRECT ANSWERS)

1.	D	11.	B
2.	C	12.	D
3.	A	13.	C
4.	B	14.	D
5.	A	15.	C
6.	A	16.	B
7.	C	17.	B
8.	C	18.	B
9.	D	19.	C
10.	C	20.	C

21. A
22. H
23. B
24. J
25. E

TEST 2

DIRECTIONS: Each question or incomplete statement is followed by several suggested answers or completions. Select the one that BEST answers the question or completes the statement. *PRINT THE LETTER OF THE CORRECT ANSWER IN THE SPACE AT THE RIGHT.*

1. Disinfectants such as chlorine and bromine reduce organic matter in pool water through a process known as   1____

    A. osmosis
    B. oxidation
    C. decomposition
    D. adsorption

2. Which of the following is NOT a typical remedy when pool water won't clear up?   2____

    A. Making sure the pool's filter valve is set to the *filter* position
    B. Adjusting flow rate through pool filter
    C. Checking for restrictions in intake and discharge lines
    D. Operating the filter for longer periods

3. Which of the following is used as an agent to settle matter suspended throughout the pool water?   3____

    A. Alum
    B. Sodium hypochlorite
    C. Magnesium sulfate
    D. Copper sulfate

4. To maintain the proper chemical balance in a swimming pool, it should generally be superchlorinated   4____

    A. twice a week
    B. once a week
    C. every 2 or 3 weeks
    D. monthly

5. What is the term for the accessory at the bottom of a pool filter that assures equal distribution of water through the filter media?   5____

    A. Recirculator
    B. Bulkhead
    C. Underdrain
    D. Distributor

6. Before painting concrete, which of the following chemicals is most appropriate for etching?   6____

    A. Caustic
    B. Benzene
    C. Trisodium phosphate
    D. Muriatic acid

7. _____ piping connects a pool's vacuum fitting to the pump suction.   7____

    A. Backwash
    B. Face
    C. Recirculating
    D. Return

8. The recommended total alkalinity for most concrete pools is in the range of _____ parts per million.   8____

    A. 40 to 100
    B. 80 to 120
    C. 100 to 150
    D. 100 to 200

9. A(n) _____ is a possible indicator of the presence of algae in pool water.

    A. unexplained rise in pH
    B. rise in stabilized chlorine
    C. decrease in pH
    D. decrease in stabilized chlorine

10. If a pool contains 2500 cubic feet of water, what is its approximate capacity in gallons?

    A. 5,000   B. 10,250   C. 18,750   D. 22,500

11. If acid material is to be added to pool water, it is generally best to add it

    A. in the morning   B. around midday
    C. in the early evening   D. at night

12. It is generally believed that of the following, the LEAST amount of eye irritation created by pool water is the result of

    A. low pH   B. chlorine
    C. dissolved alum   D. chloramines

13. In general, concrete pool surfaces may be painted once the temperature reaches a minimum temperature of _____ °F.

    A. 40   B. 50   C. 60   D. 70

14. If pressure builds up in a pool filter unit, each of the following is a recommended course of action EXCEPT checking

    A. and adjusting chlorine and pH levels
    B. surface of filter sand for crusting
    C. for algae in the pool and superchlorinating as required
    D. for air leaks in the intake line

15. Fresh, chemically untreated water that is periodically added to a pool to replace water that has been evaporated, leaked, or otherwise lost is known as

    A. floe   B. make-up water
    C. margin   D. recirculated water

16. A pH test is performed on pool water. What color indicates the ideal range for the effectiveness of chlorine in the water?

    A. Yellow   B. Orange
    C. Red   D. Purplish-red

17. The purpose of an equalizer line in a pool cleaning system is to

    A. avoid air locks that might inhibit skimming
    B. regulate the amount of circulating water that enters the system
    C. keep the surface of the water free from scum, oil, and other contaminants
    D. remove large particles to the pump strainer

18. What method of testing for chlorine residuals in a pool is generally best if one wants to measure individual chloramines?

    A. DPD test
    B. Total alkalinity test
    C. Orthotolidine color test
    D. Simple test strip

19. A pool is 20 feet wide and 38 feet long, with an average depth of 6 feet. A final temperature of 75°F is desired within 24 hours of beginning. The water temperature when heating begins is 55°F.
    Calculate the required heater output capacity (in British Thermal Units or BTU) for this job, given the following: a gallon of water weighs 8.33 pounds, and the pool is to be heated over a period of 20 hours. The total heat required is found by multiplying the gallonage by the pounds per gallon by the temperature increase desired.
    _____ BTU.

    A. 34,200   B. 248,886   C. 684,000   D. 5,697,720

20. The primary DISADVANTAGE associated with using iodine as a pool disinfectant is that it

    A. exists in a gaseous state in its pure form
    B. is much more expensive than chlorine
    C. tends to form hard deposits in the water line
    D. does not remove nitrogen from the water

21. If the pH level in a pool is too low, which of the following is a proper remedy?

    A. Add sodium bicarbonate
    B. Superchlorinate the water
    C. Thoroughly skim the pool
    D. Add muriatic acid

22. Typically, a pool heating unit will have to operate for a period of _____ hours before one can be assured of comfortable use.

    A. 6   B. 12   C. 24   D. 48

23. Which of the following steps in winterizing a pool is typically performed FIRST?

    A. Plugging outlets and inlets
    B. Vacuuming pool
    C. Lowering water level to 1 inch below skimmer
    D. Adding winterizing chemicals

24. If pool water is very hard, it may react over time to form calcium carbonate deposits at the point where the chlorinator tube enters the water line. This must be cleaned periodically with a solution of

    A. chlorinated isocyanurates
    B. hydrochloric acid
    C. calcium hypochlorite
    D. sodium hypochlorite

25. For proper chlorine function, the pH level of pool water must remain in the range of 25____
    A. 2.3-4.9 B. 5.4-6.7 C. 7.2-7.6 D. 8.0-8.6

KEY (CORRECT ANSWERS)

1. B
2. C
3. A
4. C
5. C

6. D
7. B
8. B
9. A
10. C

11. A
12. B
13. B
14. D
15. B

16. B
17. A
18. A
19. B
20. D

21. A
22. C
23. B
24. B
25. C

EXAMINATION SECTION
TEST 1

DIRECTIONS: Each question or incomplete statement is followed by several suggested answers or completions. Select the one that BEST answers the question or completes the statement. *PRINT THE LETTER OF THE CORRECT ANSWER IN THE SPACE AT THE RIGHT.*

1. Assume that the ticket agent at the bathhouse cannot dispense tickets from his machine because of a mechanical failure.
   You should authorize the ticket agent to

   A. sell tickets by hand from the bundle only
   B. stop selling tickets and await the installation of a stand-by machine
   C. collect cash from the patrons and have them escorted through the bathhouse entrance gate
   D. let the patrons deposit admission fees in a box at the bathhouse entrance gate

2. If an operator of a four-wheel drive beach buggy leaves the sand portion of a beach and neglects to disengage his forward gears when he starts to drive over area streets to the dump or drop area, he will

   A. cause his transmission to lose linkage
   B. excessively wear his emergency brake
   C. jam up his front differential
   D. seriously damage the springs of the vehicle

3. Inventories and replacement of material, supplies, and equipment required for pre-season preparation of beaches is normally scheduled to begin immediately after

   A. April 1st   B. Memorial Day
   C. Labor Day   D. New Year's Day

4. On an Emerson Resuscitator, the cylinder is considered full when the cylinder volume indicator shows AT LEAST _____ lbs. pressure per square inch or more.

   A. 900   B. 1300   C. 1800   D. 2800

5. The term *deadman,* when used in training courses for lifeguards assigned to oceanfront beaches, refers to

   A. a rope splicing tool
   B. beach cradles
   C. upland anchorage
   D. a fixed warning sign on a stone jetty

6. The appropriate arm signal for a lifeguard to give from a standing position on his tower to call for delivery of a resuscitator is:

   A. Pump one arm up and down from an overhead position
   B. Rotary motion in front of chest
   C. Arms extended up -- straight overhead
   D. Arms clasped overhead

7. The standard technique for executing the back pressure - arm lift method of artificial respiration requires the operator to adhere to a cycle consisting of a prescribed series of motions.
   This cycle should be repeated about _____ times per minute.

   A. two B. four C. six D. twelve

8. Assume that an elderly swimmer has collapsed while swimming. His friend, who is with him, states that the victim has a long history of heart failure. The victim is brought to the first aid station showing signs of shock and labored breathing.
   You should take which one of the following actions?

   A. Apply an oxygen mask tightly to the victim's face
   B. Using the resuscitator, turn on the inhalator valve and apply the face mask
   C. Get him dressed and send him to a hospital with his friend
   D. Wrap him in blankets to keep warm and give him a hot beverage

9. The symptoms of heat prostration MOST usually are:

   A. Face pale, pulse weak; perspiration profuse on forehead, face, and hands; faintness and nausea
   B. Face red, hot, and dry; pulse strong and fast, high fever; perhaps nausea
   C. Face purplish; pulse erratic; feet and hands cold
   D. Face pale; respiration rate down to six; patient violent

10. Of the following, the BEST method for controlling algae growth in outdoor swimming pools is to

    A. treat with heavy dosages of chlorine
    B. raise the pH with additional amounts of calcium carbonate
    C. apply standard rates of copper sulphate
    D. lower the pool level and add fresh water from the main

11. To improve the capabilities of swimming pool filters, a jelly-like substance called a *flock* must be deposited on the surface of the filter bed.
    The flock is formed by adding which of the following two chemicals to the water in the treatment tank?

    A. Anhydrous ammonia and sodium dichromate
    B. Aluminum sulphate and sodium carbonate
    C. Orthotolidine and copper sulphate
    D. Iodides and calcium chloride

12. Pool water returning from the center drain of an outdoor swimming pool is called the

    A. confluent B. effluent C. influent D. affluent

13. Backwashing in a conventional water treatment plant is USUALLY performed by the plant operator when the loss of head reaches _____ pounds per square inch.

    A. 3 1/2-4 B. 5 1/2-7 C. 8-10 D. 11-12

14. Most outdoor swimming pool operations have large heating boilers. These boilers have water columns with look-through water gauges, showing the water level in the boiler. The manual on maintenance and operation of heating plants and auxiliary equipment specifies that, while the boiler is in operation, the water column and gauge glass should be blown down

    A. daily   B. weekly   C. bi-weekly   D. monthly

15. Conventional gun-type oil burners used at park facilities are required to utilize as fuel

    A. #2 oil
    B. #4 oil
    C. #6 oil
    D. a kerosene mixture

16. Chlorine residual in municipally operated pools as required by the department of health shall be kept at NOT LESS THAN _____ ppm.

    A. 0.01   B. 0.25   C. 0.45   D. 1.0

17. Which of the following should be used to test the pH range (alkaline range) of swimming pool water?

    A. Ultraviolet light
    B. Iodides
    C. Orthotolodine
    D. Bromthymol blue

18. The filtration rate per square foot for a conventional filter is _____ gallons per square foot.

    A. 8   B. 6   C. 5   D. 3

19. Chlorine gas in steel cylinders is used as a sterilant in most outdoor swimming pools. If chlorine gas leaks occur from faulty connections, valve packings, etc., the STANDARD procedure for locating the leaks promptly is to use

    A. a lighted sulphur taper
    B. a soapy mixture
    C. acetone, applied with a camel hair brush
    D. concentrated ammonia

20. The MOST desirable time to apply lime to fairways on a golf course that is high in the acid range is

    A. during the rainy season
    B. after a long, dry spell
    C. in the fall or spring
    D. in late January

21. A bag of commercial fertilizer with a 10-6-4 classification on the printed face of the bag contains which of the following combination of chemicals by weight?

    A. 10% phosphoric acid, 6% nitrogen, and 4% potash
    B. 10% potash, 6% phosphoric acid, and 4% nitrogen
    C. 10% nitrogen, 6% phosphoric acid, and 4% potash
    D. 10% potash, 6% nitrogen, and 4% phosphoric acid

22. The turf on a tee with 15,000 square feet is badly worn because of traffic density and must be completely rehabilitated. You have completed the step requiring the application of a soil sterilant, and you are ready to apply nitrogen to the soil at a rate of two pounds of available nitrogen per thousand square feet.
How many 100 pound bags of 10-6-4 fertilizer must be applied to adequately supply the nitrogen requirements?

    A. 10   B. 8   C. 5   D. 3

23. According to regulations relating to lawn-making, which of the following pH ratings of fertilizer is desirable?

    A. 4.5 to 5.0   B. 5.5 to 6.0
    C. 6.5 to 7.0   D. 7.5 to 8.0

24. To facilitate photosynthesis for normal growth, grass should be mowed often enough so that clippings are

    A. equal to mowing height
    B. shorter than mowing height
    C. longer than mowing height
    D. two inches long

25. Of the following, the MOST suitable grass seed mixture for a play field is one containing Kentucky bluegrass and

    A. colonial bent   B. Bermuda grass
    C. zoysia   D. creeping red fescue

26. Red fescue is USUALLY added to a seed mixture because of its

    A. drought resistance B. fast germination
    C. slow germination   D. coarse texture

27. The four basic procedures generally considered as constituting the minimum maintenance for turf are: (1) selection of adapted grasses; (2) fertilization; (3) watering; and (4)

    A. aerification   B. mowing
    C. plugging   D. rolling

28. The BEST method for improving the soil structure of a heavily compacted playfield is to apply organic top-dressing first and then proceed with

    A. pesticide application   B. mowing and watering
    C. fertilization   D. aerification

29. A fairway should be maintained so that its width averages _____ to _____ feet.

    A. 60; 110   B. 120; 210   C. 220; 260   D. 270; 310

30. A good supplemental program to aid the grass that is already growing and to establish new grass in the thin, worn-out areas of an athletic field is

    A. overseeding   B. rolling
    C. plugging   D. watering

KEY (CORRECT ANSWERS)

1. A	11. B	21. C
2. C	12. B	22. D
3. C	13. B	23. C
4. C	14. A	24. B
5. C	15. A	25. D
6. C	16. D	26. A
7. D	17. D	27. B
8. B	18. D	28. D
9. A	19. D	29. B
10. C	20. C	30. A

TEST 2

DIRECTIONS: Each question or incomplete statement is followed by several suggested answers or completions. Select the one that BEST answers the question or completes the statement. *PRINT THE LETTER OF THE CORRECT ANSWER IN THE SPACE AT THE RIGHT.*

1. Traps are customarily surfaced with a layer of sand about _____ inches deep. 1._____
   A. 6 B. 12 C. 18 D. 24

2. A GOOD medium sandy loam for a putting green should contain _____ organic content. 2._____
   A. 5-10% B. 10-15% C. 20-30% D. 30-50%

3. In the maintenance of a putting green, the LEAST necessary piece of equipment is 3._____
   A. putting green mower   B. power sprayer
   C. aerator   D. fertilizer spreader

4. The BEST way to maintain a green so that it holds a pitched ball is by 4._____
   A. overwatering   B. good soil structure
   C. underwatering   D. high mowing

5. The surface soil on a green should be a medium sandy loam placed _____ to _____ inches deep. 5._____
   A. 2; 4 B. 4; 6 C. 8; 10 D. 12; 18

6. The BEST turf fertilizers today contain about 6._____
   A. 85% slow-release phosphorus
   B. 16% fast-release nitrogen
   C. 50% slow-release nitrogen
   D. 20% phosphorus

7. Since golf course grasses are heavy users of phosphorus, potassium, magnesium, and calcium, the BEST pH range for turf, where maximum quantities of these chemicals are available, is 7._____
   A. 4.2 to 4.8   B. 5.0 to 5.8
   C. 6.0 to 7.0   D. 7.2 to 8.2

8. Damage on golf greens and other turf areas caused by the *Fusarium nivale* fungus (snow mold) can BEST be prevented or adequately checked by treatment with 8._____
   A. ammonium methyl arsenates
   B. aluminum sulphate
   C. hydrated lime
   D. cadminates

9. To prevent snow mold, treatment should GENERALLY start 9._____
   A. in early spring   B. after a heavy rain
   C. in late winter   D. after a heavy snow

10. Chlordane is used in turf management to

   A. eradicate goose grass
   B. control brown patch
   C. grub-proof soil
   D. stimulate root growth

11. Artificial rinks have refrigerants to cool the brine which is constantly circulated through the wrought-iron pipes imbedded in the floor of the rink.
    The brine can be chilled to below zero degrees Fahrenheit because it contains a chemical salt known as

   A. sodium chloride
   B. calcium chloride
   C. calcium carbonate
   D. ammonium chloride

12. The MINIMUM ice thickness generally considered safe for ice skating on a lake or pond whose depth does not exceed 3 feet is _____ inches.

   A. 2
   B. 3
   C. 5
   D. 6

13. In the operation of an ice skating rink, prior to starting the process of ice building, the slab surface should be painted with _____ paint.

   A. white water
   B. white epoxy
   C. blue water
   D. blue epoxy

14. Crowd control in an ice skating rink includes all phases of the patrons' activities from admissions line-up to the time the patrons leave the rink.
    According to regulations, during special sessions, guards should

   A. skate in a clockwise direction
   B. skate in a counterclockwise direction
   C. be positioned on the ice near the entrances
   D. be positioned off the ice near the entrances

15. When a rink slab has been chilled below freezing temperature, ice can be built to the desired thickness by spraying a fine layer of water onto the slab with a

   A. Toro sprayer
   B. Skinner sprinkler
   C. Rainboni
   D. Zamboni

16. The following is a description of the cooling system of a skating rink: The refrigerant (ammonia or freon) absorbs the heat from the circulating brine which, in turn, lowers the temperature of the skating slab; when the brine is returned to the chiller after leaving the rink floor with absorbed heat, the compressor pumps the refrigerant gases to the condenser.
    The condenser does which of the following?
    It

   A. cools the refrigerant gas to a liquid and returns it to the chiller
   B. heats up the refrigerant gas
   C. transforms the gas into ice crystals
   D. cools the circulating water within the condenser

17. At indoor rinks where atmospheric temperatures remain stable and are not affected by outdoor weather conditions, brine should be circulated at a temperature of APPROXIMATELY _____ degrees Fahrenheit.

   A. 7
   B. 10
   C. 15
   D. 25

18. Conditioning ice surfaces on outdoor rinks in early fall or late spring is BEST accomplished

    A. after each session
    B. after the sun sets
    C. at 8 A.M.
    D. at 12 noon

19. The standard of thickness for safe skating on lakes and ponds with water depths over three feet is _____ inches.

    A. two
    B. three
    C. five
    D. seven

20. Assume that a heavy snowstorm has reached the area at the start of the evening session of outdoor rink operations. The one of the following actions that should be taken is to

    A. send all the skaters home, telling them the rink is closed
    B. let them skate until the snow is too deep to move
    C. cone off one-half of the rink at a time for snow removal operations
    D. give snow shovels to as many skaters as possible and put them to work clearing the rink

21. Of the following trees, the one which is NOT recommended for street tree planting is

    A. London plane
    B. Gingko
    C. Yellow Pine
    D. Pin Oak

22. Before useful measures can be applied to control a tree disease epidemic in a park, it is FIRST necessary to

    A. obtain an appropriation for spraying
    B. have a correct diagnosis made of the disease
    C. make an inventory of the diseased trees
    D. wait until winter when the trees are dormant

23. Of the following trees, the one which is generally MOST often recommended for sandy soils is

    A. American elm
    B. Japanese maple
    C. Chinese poplar
    D. Japanese black pine

24. About 75 percent of all tree diseases, including all mildews, rusts, anthracnoses, and sooty molds, are caused by

    A. fungi
    B. viruses
    C. nematodes
    D. bacteria

25. Tree crews should be instructed to ALWAYS

    A. trim the leader of a tree to improve its vitality
    B. prune trees by removing at least 50% of the crowns
    C. remove all injured and diseased wood
    D. fertilize a tree before pruning it

26. Three techniques that you can use to evaluate maintenance activities and determine whether they can be done better are work simplification, work measurement, and

    A. establishment of work performance standards
    B. use of labor saving devices
    C. increased supervision
    D. computerization

27. Staffing is BEST indicated by which of the following activities?

    A. Selection and training of personnel and maintaining favorable conditions of work
    B. Structuring an organization for unity of command, span of control, and lines of authority
    C. Writing task lists for the different titles working at a facility
    D. Working out in broad outline the things that need to be done and the methods for doing them to accomplish the mission of the agency

28. Generally, the MOST practical way to ascertain most readily the number of man-hours it takes to do a job is by

    A. referring to a management analysis handbook
    B. making a detailed analysis of the job
    C. asking the operator performing the job
    D. reviewing job specifications

29. Any violation of the rules or regulations for the government and protection of public parks and property shall be punishable by NOT MORE THAN _____ imprisonment or by a fine of not more than _____ dollars, or by both.

    A. thirty days'; fifty
    B. sixty days'; one hundred
    C. ninety days'; two hundred fifty
    D. one year's; five hundred

30. One workman can hand-rake leaves at the rate of approximately 1,000 square feet in 20 minutes.
    How many men would you assign to a crew to hand rake a grove of trees covering 40,000 square feet in order to accomplish the job within three hours?

    A. 3 B. 30 C. 50 D. 5

KEY (CORRECT ANSWERS)

1.	A	11.	B	21.	C
2.	C	12.	B	22.	B
3.	B	13.	A	23.	D
4.	B	14.	D	24.	A
5.	C	15.	D	25.	C
6.	C	16.	A	26.	A
7.	C	17.	C	27.	A
8.	D	18.	A	28.	C
9.	A	19.	C	29.	A
10.	C	20.	C	30.	D

EXAMINATION SECTION
TEST 1

DIRECTIONS: Each question or incomplete statement is followed by several suggested answers or completions. Select the one that BEST answers the question or completes the statement. *PRINT THE LETTER OF THE CORRECT ANSWER IN THE SPACE AT THE RIGHT.*

1. To cut a number of 2" x 4" lengths of wood accurately at an angle of 45°, it is BEST to use a

    A. coping saw
    B. mitre-box
    C. square
    D. marking gauge

2. The leverage that can be obtained with a wrench is determined MAINLY by the

    A. material of which the wrench is made
    B. gripping surface of the jaw
    C. length of the handle
    D. thickness of the wrench

3. Many electric power tools, such as drills, have a third conductor in the line cord which should be connected to a grounded part of the power receptacle.
The reason for this is to

    A. have a spare wire in case one power wire should break
    B. strengthen the power lead so that it cannot be easily damaged
    C. protect the user of the tool from electric shocks
    D. allow use of the tool for extended periods of time without overheating

4. A cold chisel whose head has become *mushroomed* should NOT be used primarily because

    A. it is impossible to hit the head squarely
    B. the chisel will not cut accurately
    C. chips might fly from the head
    D. the chisel has lost its *temper*

5. Catch basins are used in connection with

    A. buried gas mains
    B. underground springs
    C. storm water sewer systems
    D. water heaters

6. The ratio of air to gasoline in an automobile engine is controlled by the

    A. gas filter
    B. fuel pump
    C. carburetor
    D. distributor

7. Which of the following trees recommended for street planting has been greatly overused?

    A. London Plane
    B. Flowering Japanese Cherry
    C. Dawn Redwood
    D. Red Oak

19

8. Generally, during dry weather, a clay tennis court should be
   A. wet down at the end of each day's play, then well rolled early the next morning
   B. well rolled at the end of each day's play, then wet down early the next morning
   C. wet down and well rolled at the end of each day's play
   D. wet down and well rolled early each morning before play

9. The playing surface of a clay tennis court *generally* consists of
   A. silt
   B. clay, silt, and sand
   C. clay and silt
   D. silt and sand

10. Of the following, the frequency with which revenues from beaches, swimming pools, golf courses, and ice skating rinks are *normally* prepared for deposit is
    A. twice daily
    B. daily
    C. twice a week
    D. weekly

11. The one of the following which is the BEST time, as a general rule, for removing debris deposited on the beaches by the tide during the winter is
    A. every day
    B. once a week
    C. once a month
    D. only before the opening of the beaches for the summer

12. Snow fences are usually used at beaches in winter PRIMARILY to
    A. prevent snow from drifting too high near buildings
    B. prevent driftwood from coming too far up on the beaches
    C. control wind erosion of sand from the beaches
    D. temporarily replace regular fences and railings which are damaged

13. Of the following, the filter material used in all of the gravity system filters of public swimming pools is
    A. sand
    B. diatomaceous earth
    C. anthrafilt
    D. resin-impregnated paper

14. At an outdoor public rink, the PROPER procedure during a snowfall *normally* is to
    A. close half the rink at a time for snow removal, leaving the other half open for skating
    B. disregard the snow until the normal end of sessions, at which time snow should be removed and ice renovated
    C. close the rink, as snow usually creates hazardous skating conditions
    D. clear the rink, then melt the snow with a hot-water spray; skating may be resumed when the water freezes

15. If ice expands or contracts because of temperature fluctuations, large fissures or cracks can form. Such cracks *generally* are
    A. *abnormal* and an indication of thin ice conditions
    B. *normal*, but can become trip hazards, and so should be filled in
    C. *normal* and safe, and can be ignored
    D. *very common,* and the best indication of thin ice

16. According to instructions, the FIRST and MOST important duty performed each morning by every greensman at a golf course is to _____ the greens.   16._____

    A. water   B. mow   C. rake   D. whip

17. A golfer is entitled to tee off and must be ready to tee off when his number is called by the starter.   17._____
    Golfers not present or ready to tee off when their number is called will, upon returning to the starter's board, be reassigned by the starter _____ numbers below the number

    A. 10; on their ticket
    B. 10; being called at the time of their return
    C. 20; on their ticket
    D. 20; being called at the time of their return

18. Assume that a player is at a public golf course which is not a pitch-putt course, and that this golfer does not have an approved adjustable club.   18._____
    Of the following, the equipment that this player MUST have is

    A. at least three golf clubs, including a putter and one wood
    B. at least seven golf clubs, including a putter and one wood
    C. a golf bag or carrier and at least three golf clubs, one of which must be a putter
    D. a golf bar or carrier and at least seven golf clubs, including a putter and one wood

19. Ball marks on golf course greens must be repaired as they occur.   19._____
    To repair such marks before they dry out, each greensman must be equipped with a

    A. sharp table fork or penknife
    B. bamboo or wooden rake
    C. spade
    D. watering can

20. Performance of necessary maintenance on machines according to a regular schedule is generally   20._____

    A. *desirable,* primarily because the appearance of machinery should be kept up
    B. *undesirable,* primarily because it is a waste of both man-hours and machine-hours to repair functioning machinery
    C. *undesirable,* primarily because too much maintenance is as bad as not enough
    D. *desirable,* primarily because regularly maintained machinery is more efficient and less likely to suffer a major breakdown at a time when it is urgently needed

21. During your regular inspection tour, you notice a youth writing on a statue.   21._____
    Of the following, the BEST immediate action for long-range results is for you to

    A. ignore the youth, because if you indicate to him that he is wrong, he will only continue to write
    B. approach the youth and inform him that you will take him to police headquarters for breaking park department rules
    C. tell the youth that you know he has defaced property throughout the park and is prohibited by law from entering the park again
    D. talk to the youth concerning the cost of graffiti, give him a sincere but stern warning on the penalties involved, and suggest that he join a *neighborhood task force*

22. An irate citizen telephones you to state her anger about a parks department employee. She states that the employee has asked her children not to pick shrubs or flowers and the children were heartbroken because they were making a bouquet for their grandmother. The mother states that the park is for the enjoyment of the public and such action by the employee was unwarranted.
Of the following, the BEST method of handling the situation is for you to

   A. apologize for the employee by informing the citizen that he was new and did not understand children
   B. inform the caller that she will have to file a written complaint to the parks department
   C. sympathize with the caller, but tell her that park rules prohibit such action because it marks the beauty of the park
   D. tell the caller that park employees are properly trained, and always perform correctly

23. After repeated warnings by you about violation of parks department regulations, two concessionaries have had their permits revoked. The two wish to be reinstated and have asked local community groups to intervene. The groups, concerned with protecting the rights of the citizens against unwarranted actions, have come to you asking for the reasons for the revocations and for all information related to them.
Of the following, the BEST course of action for you to take for the maintenance of good public relations is to

   A. state that information concerning internal operations is confidential
   B. provide the information requested, avoiding opinions and off-the-record comments
   C. inform the groups that you do not know the reasons for the permit revocations, but you will inform them as soon as the information becomes available
   D. explain that standards are set for concessionaires and any departure from these regulations is cause for revocation

24. Assume that as a newly appointed supervisor, one of the first work orders you issue involves painting and restoring equipment in a little-used children's play area in a district park.
The one of the following which would be the MOST likely effect upon patrons who frequent such areas is that this would

   A. create better public relations, since a pleasing appearance of physical facilities helps establish confidence in the park system
   B. have no effect on public relations since the area was not often used
   C. create poor public relations since such repairs will require closing the area
   D. raise suspicions concerning the park's efficiency, since it was senseless to improve a little-used play area

25. In order to get maximum use of facilities adjacent to an outdoor pool, you have decided to open the pavilions as winter recreation centers for indoor games.
Of the following, the MOST important factor for the effectiveness of such a program is generally

   A. how well the immediate director is known and liked
   B. the amount of publicity news media give the program
   C. how well similar park programs have been accepted by the public
   D. how well the public understands and cooperates with the program

KEY (CORRECT ANSWERS)

1.	B		11.	A
2.	C		12.	C
3.	C		13.	C
4.	C		14.	A
5.	C		15.	B
6.	C		16.	D
7.	A		17.	D
8.	A		18.	C
9.	B		19.	A
10.	B		20.	D

21. C
22. B
23. C
24. A
25. C

TEST 2

DIRECTIONS: Each question or incomplete statement is followed by several suggested answers or completions. Select the one that BEST answers the question or completes the statement. *PRINT THE LETTER OF THE CORRECT ANSWER IN THE SPACE AT THE RIGHT.*

1. Assume that two very powerful community groups, who have both been very cooperative with park programs, are in disagreement concerning dogs in the park. One group insists that park rules prohibit unleashed dogs, while the other asserts that the rule has never been enforced. Of the following, the BEST course of action for you to take in order to maintain good public relations is to 1.____

    A. inform both groups that a special area of the park will be set aside for unleashed dogs
    B. tell both groups that they will have to file written complaints before any action can be taken
    C. tell the group desirous of unleashed dogs that park rules prohibit unleashed animals, but appeals for change may be made
    D. inform the group protesting unleashed dogs that, since the rules has not been strictly enforced in the past, it would be fruitless to try now

2. Assume that you are meeting with the cabinet of the local office of neighborhood government. These community representatives complain that a certain playground has been repeatedly vandalized. Your men have made repairs at this facility on several occasions. Of the following, the MOST effective advice you can give the cabinet about such a situation generally is that 2.____

    A. you are short-handed and nothing more can be done
    B. the community has a large responsibility for seeing that park facilities are not vandalized, and suggest that a community group accept responsibility for reporting all vandalism to the police
    C. the cabinet members should write a letter to the mayor
    D. the cabinet should not interfere in the administration of the parks; the parks department is best able to determine how to handle a situation involving vandalism

3. As a supervisor, you may speak to various groups or organizations about services and activities provided by the district. 3.____
    Of the following, the factor normally LEAST necessary for making a successful talk is

    A. a good idea or subject for discussion
    B. useful knowledge of your subject
    C. formal training in the techniques of public speaking
    D. a sincere desire and basic ability to express your ideas

4. You have received a letter of complaint from a local resident that a laborer in a playground in the district was rude to her and her children. You have received other complaints about this person in the past. 4.____
    In the interest of maintaining good community relations, the one of the following actions which it would normally be BEST for you to take is to

A. investigate, and promptly telephone or write an appropriate response describing what action, if any, you have taken and send a report to the local office
B. investigate, and send a report to the local office to let the local office decide if any action is appropriate
C. dismiss the letter as the work of a chronic crank and do nothing; to investigate might annoy your man
D. file the complaint so that if several similar ones come in, you can take appropriate action in the future

5. Which of the following is MOST likely to project an unfavorable impression of a municipal agency?
If you are

   A. making a telephone call, identify yourself and the organization immediately
   B. dealing with the public, try to make the people feel important
   C. making a visit, do not hesitate to leave your car improperly parked
   D. delivering supplies, obey the speed limit and stay in the right lane when not passing

6. Of the following, two factors upon which good public relations for a municipal agency depend are favorable media coverage and generally

   A. a good service performance record
   B. the scope of services to be provided
   C. the magnitude of the annual budget
   D. the type of equipment used

7. Several groups interested in determining a location for the new baseball diamond have presented their preferences to you. Rather than yield to the loudest group, you have asked the interested groups to make their requests based on facts such as size, accessibility, number of trees that would have to be destroyed, etc.
Of the following, the BEST reason for making your decision based on these factors is that

   A. facts are always easy to obtain
   B. the decision has a basis which can be defended by interested parties
   C. by this method, the loudest group doesn't always win
   D. you can never go wrong by using facts

8. If a person who is using a park facility is treated discourteously by a park employee, the offended person is *generally* likely to think ill of

   A. just that employee
   B. just that employee and his supervisor
   C. the parks department and the city or county
   D. just the park where the incident took place

9. If a member of the public is seen violating one of the park rules and regulations, the BEST way to stop the person from continuing is generally to

A. shout loudly at the person, so that he and all others who have seen him will know that his actions violate park rules
B. approach the person courteously, tell him of his violation, and be willing to answer any question he may have about the rules
C. inform the person that he is in violation of the rules and must leave the park facilities at once
D. ignore the violation, since park personnel do not want the reputation of acting like policemen

10. Park rules and regulations exist to insure that the greatest number of people make the best use of park facilities. Of the following, the responsibility for seeing that the public follows the rules and regulations falls PRIMARILY on

    A. the supervisor alone, since he is usually the highest ranking person
    B. both the supervisor and the park foreman, since they are supervisory personnel
    C. all park employees who have contact with the public
    D. parks department administrators since they are the ones who establish park priorities

11. The one of the following requirements which is usually necessary for signs to be effective in informing the public of a park regulation is that

    A. the bottom of signs be no more than 4 1/2 feet from the ground
    B. there be as many of the same type of sign as possible
    C. the signs be legibly lettered, with correct spelling and wording
    D. the signs be distributed at random around the park facility

12. If a lifeguard at a public beach or pool gives one long blast on his whistle, he is

    A. signaling that he is leaving his station in response to an emergency situation
    B. calling the attention of the public to violations of rules and regulations
    C. calling for the attention of the lifeguard chief or lieutenant (not an emergency)
    D. signaling that he is going off duty, and another lifeguard should cover his station

13. The one of the following conditions which is LEAST necessary to insure that the public uses rubbish baskets is that the baskets be

    A. in good physical condition
    B. emptied when full
    C. conspicuously located
    D. distributed randomly throughout the park area

14. If a park facility is kept clean and well-maintained, the rate of vandlism will likely

    A. *be lowered,* since public cooperation is induced by well-kept facilities
    B. *be raised,* since vandals prefer to damage a well-kept area
    C. *remain the same,* since the upkeep of a facility has no effect on the rate of vandalism
    D. *be raised,* since a well-kept facility is easier to damage than a poorly-kept facility

15. In addition to planned regular maintenance, the one of the following which is the best way to keep park facilities at a high level of operating efficiency so the public may have the GREATEST use of the facilities is usually to

   A. make frequent and thorough inspections of all facilities followed by corrective measures when needed
   B. wait for complaints from park facility users since manpower is wasted by correcting defects normally unnoticed by the public
   C. take corrective action only on complaints made to the borough offices, since only these need be considered serious
   D. disregard most complaints, since regular maintenance corrects all serious defects in park facilities

Directions 16-25.

DIRECTIONS: Questions 16 through 25 are to be answered on the basis of the information given below and the two tables which follow. Some of the questions require taking into consideration the information in one or both of the two tables and in the following paragraphs. No question relates to a previous question.

As a General Park Foreman, R. Carson has been newly assigned to Undulant Memorial Park, District 841. The schedules have been made up by the previous General Park Foreman for the week of June 30 to July 6. The park has 500 acres of grass, a wooded picnic area of 200 acres, 4 comfort stations, a surfaced playground area for children, 10 tennis courts, 2 baseball diamonds, 4 softball diamonds, 6 basketball courts, and 100 acres of additional wooded area which are being converted to picnic grounds. The conversion of the wooded area is to be completed before July 4th.

The roster of personnel assigned to District 841 includes 1 General Park Foreman, 2 Park Foremen, 9 laborers, 4 attendants (whose activities are restricted to the tennis courts and locker rooms), and 12 seasonal park helpers. The equipment assigned to District 841 includes 1 pickup truck, 1 dump truck, 1 tractor and grass cutting attachment, 2 Toro mowers, and 2 hand mowers.

The operating requirements (weekly scheduled operations which must be met) for District 841 include a daily morning garbage pickup for the picnic area, a twice weekly pickup Monday and Friday for the rest of the District, and a weekly walking pickup of the entire area on Thursday (see Table II). A garbage pickup of the picnic area takes 4 hours and requires the use of 3 men and a dump truck. The garbage pickup for the rest of the district requires the use of that crew for an additional 3 hours. The walking pickup takes 8 hours and requires the use of 6 men and a pickup truck.

The <u>hours of operation</u> for all facilities in District 841 are <u>8 A.M. to 9 P.M.</u> Seasonal park helpers are scheduled to work 6 days per week, and employees in all other titles are scheduled to work 5 days per week. One hour is given for lunch or supper.

TABLE I

TIME SCHEDULE Periods: From June 23 to June 29
Dept. of Parks   Park: Undulant Memorial Park
District 841

Title	Sat. 6/23	Sun. 6/24	Mon. 6/25	Tues. 6/26	Wed. 6/27	Thurs. 6/28	Fri. 6/29
General Park Foreman	8-5	8-5	8-5	8-5	8-5		
Park Foreman		8-5	8-5	8-5		8-5	8-5
Park Foreman	1-9		1-9		1-9	1-9	1-9
Laborers 3*	8-5			8-5	8-5	8-5	8-5
Laborers 3		8-5	8-5	8-5	8-5	8-5	
Laborers 3	1-9		1-9		1-9	1-9	1-9
Seasonal Park Helper 3	8-5		8-5	8-5	8-5	8-5	8-5
Seasonal Park Helper 3		8-5	8-5	8-5	8-5	8-5	8-5
Seasonal Park Helper 3	1-9		1-9	1-9	1-9	1-9	1-9
Seasonal Park Helper 3		1-9	1-9	1-9	1-9	1-9	1-9
Attendant 2	10-6	10-6	10-6	10-6	10-6		
Attendant 2	10-6	10-6			10-6	10-6	10-6

LEGEND
*Number of employees in that title on that time schedule
8-5 Tour of duty from 8 A.M. to 5 P.M. (8-hour shift)
1-9 Tour of duty from 1 P.M. to 9 P.M. (7-hour shift)
10-6 Tour of duty from 10 A.M. to 6 P.M. (7-hour shift)

TABLE II

OPERATING REQUIREMENTS

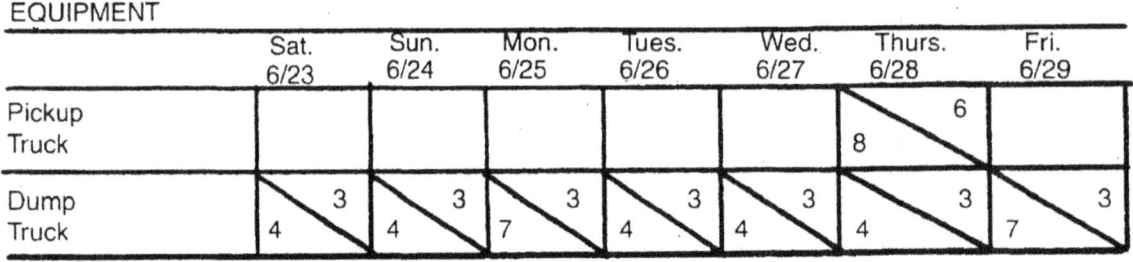

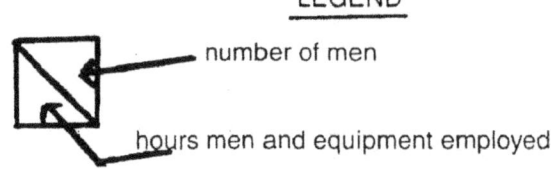

LEGEND
number of men
hours men and equipment employed

16. A man using the tractor with grass-cutting equipment can cut an average of ten acres of grass per hour; with a Toro mower, 4 acres per hour; and with a hand mower, 1 acre per hour. Only 250 of the 500 acres of grass can be cut with the tractor.
    The total number of <u>man-hours</u> (one man-hour is defined as one hour of work for one man) it will take to cut all 500 acres of grass using all the available machinery simultaneously is MOST NEARLY

    A. 50 B. 100 C. 125 D. 200

17. The conversion of the wooded area to picnic grounds is complete except for the installation of 100 additional picnic tables. It is estimated that this project requires the use of a pickup truck and 2 men for 40 hours. Because this is a priority item, it will be worked on during all the hours the park is open.
    If the project must be completed by Friday noon for the 4th of July holiday, considering that the operating requirements listed in Table II must be met, we would expect the project to begin

    A. Saturday afternoon   B. Sunday morning
    C. Monday afternoon   D. Tuesday afternoon

18. Assuming that all the operating requirements must be met, of the following, the day on which there will NOT be a sufficient number of men available to install baseball and softball backstops, a project requiring the simultaneous use of 8 men for 7 hours is

    A. Saturday B. Monday C. Thursday D. Friday

19. It has become obvious that the dump truck is in need of repairs. These repairs will take two days, during which time the truck cannot be used. However, the pickup truck can be substituted for the dump truck in picking up the garbage, but requires twice the time to perform this operation.
    Of the following, the day on which the dump truck should be entered for repairs, if the operating requirements are to be met, is

    A. Monday B. Tuesday C. Wednesday D. Thursday

20. Excluding the General Park Foreman and the Park Foremen, attendants, and those scheduled for a garbage pickup, the number of man-hours available for assignment on Monday is

    A. 79 B. 105 C. 114 D. 135

21. The number of man-hours expended in meeting the operating requirements during the one-week period ending June 29 is

    A. 130 B. 150 C. 200 D. 250

22. In making out the schedule for this week, the previous General Park Foreman neglected to assign enough men for Sunday, June 24, to set up benches for a concert to be given the following Monday. It is estimated that this project requires 85 man-hours and must be completed by closing hours Sunday evening.
    To complete this project and fulfill the operating requirements, the number of ADDITIONAL men for an 8-5 (8 hour) shift that must be reassigned to work on Sunday is

    A. 1 B. 2 C. 3 D. 4

23. There is a 120-acre section of grass which requires earlier than usual cutting because of its low-lying well-watered location. This section can only be cut by the Toro power mowers, which cut four acres per hour, and the hand mowers, which cut one acre per hour. Assume that one of the Toro power mowers is in the repair shop. The number of ADDITIONAL hours it will take to cut this 120-acre section of grass using the remaining grass-cutting machinery (in comparison with using all of the Toro power mowers and hand mowers) is

   A. 8   B. 10   C. 12   D. 20

24. Of those laborers and seasonal park helpers scheduled to work on Friday, the percentage that is employed in fulfilling the operating requirements is MOST NEARLY

   A. 8.2   B. 16.6   C. 23.8   D. 37.5

25. For scheduling purposes, the General Park Foreman must know how long it will take to complete the garbage collection on Monday, June 25, if both the dump truck and the pickup truck are used.
   If the pickup truck takes twice as long as the dump truck in collecting garbage, the number of hours it takes to collect the garbage using both trucks is MOST NEARLY

   A. 2.1   B. 3.2   C. 4.7   D. 6.3

KEY (CORRECT ANSWERS)

1. C		11. C	
2. B		12. A	
3. C		13. D	
4. A		14. A	
5. C		15. A	
6. A		16. C	
7. B		17. C	
8. C		18. A	
9. B		19. B	
10. C		20. C	

21. B
22. D
23. A
24. B
25. C

EXAMINATION SECTION
TEST 1

DIRECTIONS: Each question or incomplete statement is followed by several suggested answers or completions. Select the one that BEST answers the question or completes the statement. *PRINT THE LETTER OF THE CORRECT ANSWER IN THE SPACE AT THE RIGHT.*

1. McArthur Park's lawn area covers approximately 6,000 sq. ft., all of which needs to be fertilized. You are using 25-4-6 fertilizer. _____ pounds of fertilizer is the CORRECT amount needed to apply four pounds of nitrogen per 1,000 sq. ft.
    A. 16   B. 60   C. 96   D. 120

    1._____

2. The Municipality of Anchorage Public Works Department's work schedule is split into 8-hour days with 5 crews working each day. Each group is made up of the following personnel: 1 supervisor, 3 equipment operators, 5 laborers. You are putting together the schedule and need to account for all the laborer hours per 8-hour shift. Which of the following are the total laborer hours per 8-hour work day?
    A. 150   B. 25   C. 200   D. 40

    2._____

3. Your crew is tasked with constructing a baseball mound. One of the members of your crew starts to lay down sand at the foundation. You know this is the wrong material to use because she should be using which of the following materials to construct the mound correctly?
    A. Concrete
    B. Screened clay
    C. Loam
    D. None of the above

    3._____

4. The Bismarck Parks and Recreation Department is remodeling and repurposing a previously abandoned building over the winter. When the work crew arrives at the building, they immediately notice a strong sewer gas smell. Which one of the following is MOST likely the reason for the strong smell?
    A. The plumbing vents are covered in snow.
    B. The pipes are overly dry, leading to a buildup of gas.
    C. Ice has gotten into the plumbing.
    D. The windows just need to be opened.

    4._____

5. A new worker is attempting to push the reset button on one of the park's garbage disposals. The garbage disposal in question is a standard edition, so the reset button should be located
    A. in the breaker box
    B. on the outlet nearest the disposal
    C. on the nearest wall
    D. on the bottom of the disposal

    5._____

6. Your crew is tasked with cleaning up a latex paint spill at a facility. Which of the following would BEST help you clean the paint?
   A. Turpentine   B. Goo-B-Gone   C. Water   D. Varsal

7. Which of the following mineral nutrients is required in the greatest amount for the growth and survival of lawn grasses?
   A. Nitrogen   B. Potassium   C. Calcium   D. Phosphorus

8. Your crew is scheduled to maintain a park lawn that is mostly made up of fescue grass. When you meet with your laborers, you remind them that the lawn should be cut to a height of _____ inches.
   A. 1-2   B. 2-3   C. ½-1   D. ¾-1½

9. When is the preferred time of day to water the lawn?
   A. Morning   B. Evening   C. Midday   D. Late at night

10. A park's grass is not growing well, and you find out it is due to a lack of deep roots. You explain to the crews working on the park that they need to water the lawn
    A. heavily and often
    B. lightly and often
    C. heavily and infrequently
    D. lightly and infrequently

11. While at work one day, you notice a damp patch on a wall. What should you do?
    A. Ignore it. When the weather gets better, the damp patch will go away.
    B. Take some paint or new wallpaper and cover up the patch.
    C. Check the gutters, downpipes, and drains to make sure they are working properly.
    D. Scrape away the damp patch. Mud over the area and apply paint afterwards.

12. Arriving at the park one day, you notice ivy is growing all over a nearby wall on a building. What should you do?
    A. Cut through the ivy stems at the base and remove the ivy from the wall once the plant is dead.
    B. Take the ivy off the wall immediately.
    C. Use a weed killer to kill the ivy at its root.
    D. If the ivy is causing no damage at present and the wall is in good condition, leave it as is.

13. If the United States officially identifies a site without prejudice to national sovereignty or ownership, and constitutes a unique natural or cultural resource and for whose protection it is the duty of the international community as a whole to cooperate, it is better known as a(n)
    A. national park
    B. area of International Conservation
    C. World Heritage Place
    D. none of the above

14. The last two years has seen a sharp increase in injuries to children at the John Adams State Park playground. You are tasked with ensuring a way that less children are hurt at the playground this year. Which of the following actions would be the MOST effective way to keep injuries down?
    A. Discard old equipment and purchase safer, newer equipment.
    B. Perform safety inspections regularly at the facility.
    C. Move equipment farther apart from each other on the playground, thus creating more physical space.
    D. Maintain proper surfaces.

14.____

15. You are purchasing chemicals for the pools in anticipation of the community center opening during the summer. Because you know you will be audited, under which line item should you put this in your budget?
    A. Maintenance and repairs   B. Charitable funds
    C. Supplies and materials   D. None of the above

15.____

16. Which of the following should LEAST influence your public image and relations?
    A. Camp participants   B. The public
    C. Media   D. Employees

16.____

17. Why is it important to evaluate programs upon their completion?
    A. To determine if the program should continue or not
    B. To decide if participants liked the program
    C. To see if the supervisor was satisfactory
    D. To figure out if program objectives were met

17.____

18. You are about to break ground on a new playground for the park. Two days before you are set to start, you receive an e-mail stating that plans need to be changed. You reply that if the construction contract needs to be revised, then your supervisor needs to receive which of the following official documents?
    A. A change order   B. A contract modification
    C. A requisition   D. A whole new contract

18.____

19. Jonny is a potential camp participant that has a physical disability. As his parents sign him up, what kind of barriers to participation should they be warned about?
    A. You have limited financial resources to help deal with Jonny.
    B. The architectural design and construction of the camp area may be difficult for Jonny.
    C. There may be an absence of activity choices for him.
    D. Your staff may be ill equipped to work with Jonny.

19.____

20. An HVAC's economizer has two clear benefits. They save lots of energy and
    A. the building gains ideal chiller capacity
    B. there is less refrigeration loss
    C. there is less wear on the parts in motion
    D. noised with multiple frequencies is limited

20.____

21. Which of the following is a heating system that uses a refrigeration cycle?   21.____
    A. Heat pump B. Heating pipe
    C. Complete energy system D. Immersion system

22. Recently, park employees have been complaining about the air quality   22.____
    of the main building they use when forced indoors due to inclement weather.
    You are tasked with finding a way to improve the building's air quality. Which
    of the following would be the PRIMARY way to do that?
    A. Ensure a no-smoking policy is observed through the building.
    B. Educate staff, parents, and children about the materials used in the
       building.
    C. Diminish the amount of outside air drawn into the building.
    D. Maintain acceptable temperature and relative humidity.

23. The default setting for fan performance data is based on which of the   23.____
    following?
    A. Constant size and speed B. Temperature and altitude
    C. 70 degree, dry air, at 14.7 psi D. Humid air at 60 degrees

24. Which of the following is the BEST reason to inspect roofs on a continual   24.____
    basis?
    A. To ensure bird nests are not in the way
    B. To obtain watertight integrity
    C. To check for materials
    D. To look for foreign objects

25. The part of the roof that balances the pressure between the roof membrane   25.____
    and the atmosphere is the
    A. cleating B. parapet coping
    C. edge venting D. platform frame

KEY (CORRECT ANSWERS)

1.	D	11.	C
2.	C	12.	D
3.	B	13.	A
4.	A	14.	D
5.	D	15.	C
6.	C	16.	B
7.	A	17.	D
8.	B	18.	A
9.	A	19.	B
10.	B	20.	C

21. A
22. D
23. C
24. B
25. C

TEST 2

DIRECTIONS: Each question or incomplete statement is followed by several suggested answers or completions. Select the one that BEST answers the question or completes the statement. *PRINT THE LETTER OF THE CORRECT ANSWER IN THE SPACE AT THE RIGHT.*

1. Type W gypsum wallboards are primarily used for high-moisture areas such as
   A. bathrooms and utility rooms
   B. rooms with a fireplace and furnace rooms
   C. kitchens and sheds
   D. all of the above

   1.____

2. Which of the following is NOT a common roofing problem to be on the lookout for?
   A. Lifting   B. Fissuring   C. Blistering   D. Cracking

   2.____

3. The new main Parks and Recreation Office is currently being built and you are in charge of window installation. Which of the following window types would MOST likely be installed in the commercial building?
   A. Wood   B. Vinyl   C. Fiberglass   D. Steel

   3.____

4. You get a call on the radio that an emergency is in progress. In this emergency situation, who should you contact FIRST and MOST importantly?
   A. Life safety support personnel
   B. A senior manager
   C. Occupants who may be in danger
   D. Building security personnel

   4.____

5. Proper maintenance of equipment creates which of the following?
   A. Unbalanced work flow   B. Higher numbers of complaints
   C. Longer shelf life for equipment   D. Less need for employee training

   5.____

6. Which of the following would be considered a "live load" on a building?
   A. Human occupants   B. Furniture
   C. Permanent partitions   D. A and B only

   6.____

7. If you are scheduling the repair work for equipment failure, what should you base your list on?
   A. Urgency and priority
   B. Life cycle cost
   C. Established maintenance schedules
   D. Availability of workers

   7.____

8. Materials that restrict heat transfer are better known as
   A. energy obstructions   B. thermal insulators
   C. polyvinyl chlorides   D. U-factor materials

   8.____

9. When selecting the proper flooring for your new Parks and Recreation volunteer office, which of the following criterion should you use?
   A. Function   B. Cost   C. Durability   D. Safety

10. Which of the following factors differentiates the four types of roofing asphalt?
    A. Deck slope
    B. Hardness
    C. Building height
    D. Softening point

11. You tell your subordinates to fix a hairline crack in a concrete building within the park district. One of your employees asks you why the cracks need to be repaired since they pose no danger of structural damage. You tell him it will improve the building's appearance and
    A. reduce the chance of mold growth
    B. increase the size of the cracks
    C. protect against moisture penetration
    D. remove the need for monitoring the cracks later on

12. Which of the following are advantages of precast concrete?
    A. Camber in beams and slabs
    B. Reduced construction time
    C. Small margin for error
    D. Cranes required to lift panels

13. If you want your cleaning staffs to operate at optimal levels, which of the following should you make sure they are equipped with?
    A. Base of operations
    B. Proper equipment
    C. Updated uniforms and ID's
    D. All of the above

14. A door detection system and emergency lighting are examples of which of the following equipment types?
    A. Peripheral
    B. Code-required
    C. Hoistway
    D. Control

15. Which of the following is the technical term for the miniature drawing that has exact representation of the actual building?
    A. Technical   B. Riser   C. Scaled   D. Projection

16. You are called into the workout facility at the park because every time the women's locker room showers are turned on, water comes down into the men's locker room on the floor below. What is the probable cause of this issue?
    A. The shower drain pipe is leaking
    B. There is a leak in the pipe between the director and showerhead
    C. The shower curtains are not installed properly
    D. All of the above

17. What is a swagging tool used for?
    A. When you need to enlarge copper tubing
    B. When you need to connect PVC pipe joints
    C. When you need to join electrical wires
    D. None of the above

18. One of your heaters has its pilot light unable to stay lit. What part probably needs to be fixed?
    A. Ignitor
    B. Thermocouple
    C. Thermometer
    D. Ignition

18.____

19. British Thermal Units (also known as BTU's) are used to describe the amount of energy needed to cool or heat one pound of water by one degree Fahrenheit. How many BTU's are in a half ton?
    A. 10,000
    B. 6,000
    C. 8,000
    D. 12,000

19.____

20. Jerry is about to start repairs on a breaker. Since he is responsible and safe, which of the following did he make sure he did FIRST before starting any other aspect of the repair?
    A. Jerry removed the breaker.
    B. He shut off the breaker.
    C. He turned off the main line breaker.
    D. None of the above

20.____

21. In reference to roofing, what is a square measurement an area of?
    A. 10 ft. x 10 ft.
    B. 1 ft. x 1 ft.
    C. 100 ft. x 100 ft.
    D. 1000 in. x 1000 in.

21.____

22. Your work crew is in charge of retiling a hallway that leads to an indoor recreational facility with 4 in. x 4 in. ceramic tiles. If the entryway has a 120 square foot area, how many tiles would it take to cover it?
    A. 480
    B. 1,200
    C. 360
    D. 1,080

22.____

23. You need to lower the pH level in the community pool. Which of the following should you use to help do that?
    A. Sodium carbonate
    B. Chlorinated isocyanurates
    C. Muriatic acid
    D. Lactic acid

23.____

24. If a representative of a company tells you orally that they will cover something that is not covered in the written service warranty of a product, and later the management states they never agreed to pay for any service repairs, what is the oral term from the representative which is NOT stated in the service warranty referred to as?
    A. A word-of-mouth warranty
    B. Parol evidence
    C. Implied warranty
    D. Unethical

24.____

25. You have a facility that constantly has a pest problem, so you sign an agreement with a local pest control company to help take care of the issue. The city has a centralized purchasing department that executes all service contracts, which is known as what type of authority?
    A. Delegated
    B. Implied
    C. Law of agency
    D. Apparent

25.____

KEY (CORRECT ANSWERS)

1.	A		11.	C
2.	B		12.	B
3.	D		13.	D
4.	C		14.	A
5.	C		15.	C
6.	D		16.	D
7.	A		17.	A
8.	B		18.	B
9.	A		19.	B
10.	D		20.	C

21. A
22. D
23. C
24. B
25. D

EXAMINATION SECTION
TEST 1

DIRECTIONS: Each question or incomplete statement is followed by several suggested answers or completions. Select the one that BEST answers the question or completes the statement. *PRINT THE LETTER OF THE CORRECT ANSWER IN THE SPACE AT THE RIGHT.*

1. Of the following, wood formwork for an 8' x 8' rectangular reinforced concrete footing is BEST braced

    A. by stakes driven into the ground adjacent to the form-work
    B. at the corners of the framework with vertical wooden cleats
    C. by metal form ties tieing into walers
    D. by external diagonal wood members bearing against the ground

    1.____

2. The depth of formwork for a 2'0" deep footing bearing on earth should be MOST NEARLY

    A. 2'0"   B. 2'3"   C. 3'0"   D. 3'3"

    2.____

3. Two adjacent walls are to have 1/2 inch solid expansion joint material between them. Of the following, the MOST practical method is to

    A. pour the walls, chop out 1/2 inch of concrete, and insert the expansion joint material
    B. pour one wall, anchor the expansion joint material to the poured wall, and use this as a form for the second wall
    C. nail the expansion joint material to the formwork of the first wall and pour the wall
    D. insert the expansion joint material in the space provided after the walls are poured

    3.____

4. Hollow tile masonry units are provided with their characteristic cells or voids in order to

    A. allow for packing with greater quantities of mortar
    B. provide paths for better wall drainage
    C. provide space for piping to run through
    D. achieve reduction in the weight of the units

    4.____

5. The difference between quicklime and hydrated lime, as far as the addition of water is concerned, is that

    A. hydrated lime requires soaking only
    B. quicklime requires soaking only
    C. hydrated lime requires soaking and slaking
    D. quicklime requires slaking only

    5.____

6. Cinder concrete is used in floor slabs rather than stone concrete PRIMARILY because cinder concrete

    A. has greater strength   B. is easier to place
    C. will not honeycomb   D. weighs less

    6.____

7. *Grounds* are used to

   A. guide in bringing plaster to an even surface
   B. raise flooring off damp soil
   C. prevent electrical connections from touching walls
   D. support brick walls

8. Ceramic tile is tile made of

   A. inorganic chemical plastic
   B. clay
   C. cement and sand
   D. asphalt and sand

9. Of the following species of lumber, the one MOST likely to be used for wood formwork for concrete is

   A. pine   B. birch   C. maple   D. oak

10. A concrete column measures 3'0" square at the base, tapers uniformly to 2'0" square at the top, and is 14'0" high.
    The volume of concrete required for this column, in cubic feet, is MOST NEARLY

    A. 85   B. 90   C. 95   D. 100

11. The inspector is required to hold a number of test cylinders of concrete brought on the job.
    These cylinders will be used to test the strength of concrete in

    A. compression   B. tension
    C. shear   D. bond

12. A definite procedure of preparing test cylinders of concrete is specified.
    Of the following, the BEST reason for specifying this procedure is that it provides

    A. a basis for comparing the strength of the concrete in the cylinders tested
    B. the strongest possible cylinders
    C. the weakest possible cylinders
    D. that the inspector use extreme care in preparing the test cylinders

13. Which of the following joints in brickwork is a struck joint?

14. Portland cement mortar is gauged with hydrated lime PRIMARILY in order that it shall have

    A. better weather resistance
    B. a cleaner color
    C. more workability
    D. a quicker set

15. In foundation work, an example of a rock that would be considered a SOFT rock is

    A. gneiss   B. granite   C. shale   D. limestone

16. Segregation in concrete will result from improper

    A. curing
    B. placing
    C. formwork
    D. finishing

17. Where vinyl tile is to be laid directly upon a concrete floor, the finish on the concrete surface should be

    A. wood floated
    B. broomed
    C. steel trowelled
    D. darbied

18. An excavation for a concrete footing to support a steel column was accidentally dug 4" too deep.
    Of the following, the BEST practice would be to

    A. make the footing 4" thicker
    B. backfill the 4" with stone
    C. backfill the 4" with clean sand and puddle the fill carefully
    D. lower the footing 4"

19. The MOST common finish for a concrete walk is a _____ finish.

    A. steel trowel
    B. screeded
    C. sealed
    D. wood float

Questions 20-22.

DIRECTIONS: Questions 20 through 22 are to be answered on the basis of the following paragraph.

All cement work contracts, more or less, in setting. The contraction in concrete walls and other structures causes fine cracks to develop at regular intervals. The tendency to contract increases in direct proportion to the quantity of cement in the concrete. A rich mixture will contract more than a lean mixture. A concrete wall, which has been made of a very lean mixture and which has been built by filling only about one foot in depth of concrete in the form each day will frequently require close inspection to reveal the cracks.

20. According to the above paragraph,

    A. shrinkage seldom occurs in concrete
    B. shrinkage occurs only in certain types of concrete
    C. by placing concrete at regular intervals, shrinkage may be avoided
    D. it is impossible to prevent shrinkage

21. According to the above paragraph, the one of the factors which reduces shrinkage in concrete is the

    A. volume of concrete in wall
    B. height of each day's pour
    C. length of wall
    D. length and height of wall

22. According to the above paragraph, a rich mixture

    A. pours the easiest
    B. shows the largest amount of cracks
    C. is low in cement content
    D. need not be inspected since cracks are few

23. In the finishing of Keene's cement plaster, it is BEST to

    A. complete all troweling before the final set
    B. obtain desired finish by rubbing with carborundum block after final set
    C. trowel once before final set and water trowel after set
    D. brush with clean water and trowel to an uneven surface before final set

24. Air entraining materials are sometimes used in concrete mixes.
The BEST reason for this is that it

    A. reduces the need for the use of vibrators
    B. increases the resistance to frost action
    C. produces a lightweight concrete
    D. eliminates honeycombing

25. Vermiculite plaster is used instead of the standard sand-lime plaster to

    A. reduce the dead load
    B. make a soundproof structure
    C. make the structure vermin-proof
    D. make a fireproof structure

KEY (CORRECT ANSWERS)

1.	D	11.	A
2.	B	12.	A
3.	C	13.	B
4.	D	14.	C
5.	A	15.	C
6.	D	16.	B
7.	A	17.	C
8.	B	18.	A
9.	A	19.	D
10.	B	20.	D

21. B
22. B
23. C
24. B
25. A

TEST 2

DIRECTIONS: Each question or incomplete statement is followed by several suggested answers or completions. Select the one that BEST answers the question or completes the statement. *PRINT THE LETTER OF THE CORRECT ANSWER IN THE SPACE AT THE RIGHT.*

1. A desirable quality of a concrete foundation wall is a smooth, even surface. To obtain this result, the

    A. faces of the forms must be oiled before the concrete is placed
    B. concrete must be worked next to the form faces with a spading tool
    C. forms must be made of plywood
    D. concrete placed at the form faces must contain more water than the concrete placed in the center of the forms

    1.___

2. The APPROXIMATE dimensions of a common brick are as shown. The volume of the brick, in cubic feet, is

    A. 64
    B. 5 1/3
    C. 4/9
    D. 1/27

    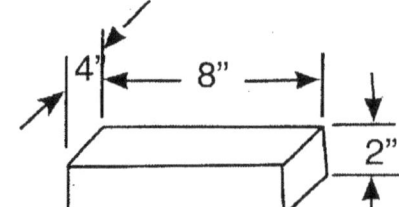

    2.___

3. When wooden forms used in concrete work are taken down, the nails in the lumber, which is saved for future use are removed rather than bent over and clinched.
The purpose of this procedure is to

    A. prevent the old nails from being unbent and used again
    B. prevent the possible staining of the concrete by contact with rusty nails
    C. avoid damage to the saw if the lumber is cut
    D. permit future use of the same nail holes

    3.___

4. A portion of a specification states: Concrete, other than that placed under water, should be compacted and worked into place by spading or puddling.
The MAIN reason why spading and puddling is required is to

    A. insure that all water in the concrete mix is brought to the surface
    B. eliminate stone pockets and large bubbles of air
    C. provide a means to obtain a spade full of concrete for test purposes
    D. make allowances for bleeding and segregation of the concrete

    4.___

5. Assume that the following statement appears in a construction contract: Payment will be made for the number of pounds of bar reinforcement incorporated in the work as shown on the plans.
This type of contract is MOST likely

    A. cost plus   B. lump sum
    C. subcontract   D. unit price

    5.___

6. According to the building code, masonry footings shall extend at least 4' below finished grade.
   The PRIMARY reason for this is to

   A. get below the frost line
   B. make the foundation stronger
   C. keep water out of the basement
   D. reach a lower soil strata where better bearing material can be found

7. The number of days that it will take high early strength concrete to equal the 28-day strength of normal portland cement concrete is MOST NEARLY

   A. 1   B. 3   C. 7   D. 12

8. Of the following devices, the one that is LEAST frequently used to attach a piece of equipment to concrete or masonry walls is a(n)

   A. carriage bolt   B. through bolt
   C. lag screw   D. expansion bolt

Questions 9-10.

DIRECTIONS: Questions 9 and 10 refer to the mortar joints shown below.

9. The mortar joint MOST frequently used on common brickwork is

   A. 1   B. 2   C. 3   D. 4

10. The mortar joint which would NOT usually be made unless an outside scaffold was used is

    A. 1   B. 2   C. 3   D. 4

11. Joints on interior surfaces of brick walls are usually flush joints EXCEPT when the walls are to be

    A. painted   B. plastered
    C. waterproofed   D. dampproofed

12. The headers in a brick veneer wall serve

    A. both a structural and an architectural purpose
    B. a structural purpose *only*
    C. an architectural purpose *only*
    D. no structural or architectural purpose

13. On a drawing, the standard cross-section shown at the right represents MOST NEARLY

    A. sand
    B. concrete
    C. earth
    D. rock

14. Specifications covering brickwork usually require special precautions and protection for work in cold weather.
    The highest temperature below which these measures are required is MOST NEARLY _____ °F.

    A. 50   B. 40   C. 30   D. 20

15. Controlled concrete is required for the reinforced concrete frame of a large building. The ultimate strength of this concrete will be MOST NEARLY _____ pounds per square inch.

    A. 1000   B. 3000   C. 5000   D. 7000

16. Concrete (a mixture of cement, sand, and coarse aggregate), if made from 1 part of one material, 3 parts of a second material, and 5 parts of the remaining material, is known as 1:3:5 concrete.
    It would be LOGICAL to conclude that the parts would be 1 _____, 3 _____, 5 _____.

    A. cement; coarse aggregate; sand
    B. coarse aggregate; cement; sand
    C. sand; coarse aggregate; cement
    D. cement; sand; coarse aggregate

17. Concrete weighs 150 pounds per cubic foot.
    A slab of concrete 6'0" long by 3'6" wide by 1'4" thick weighs MOST NEARLY _____ pounds.

    A. 4150   B. 4200   C. 4250   D. 4300

18. A post or shore is to be placed midway between columns to support the formwork for a reinforced concrete girder. The post should be cut

    A. short so that wedging is required
    B. to exact length
    C. long so that it will have to be driven into place
    D. in two pieces, to permit jackknifing into place

19. Curing of concrete would be MOST critical when the temperature and humidity are, respectively,

    A. 75° and 80%   B. 80° and 90%
    C. 85° and 10%   D. 90° and 95%

20. A specification requires that brick be laid with *shoved* joints. 20.____
    The BEST reason for this requirement is that it helps the bricklayer to obtain _____ joint(s).

    A. full
    B. plumb vertical
    C. level horizontal
    D. the required thickness of

21. If there is a small amount of water on the surface of a newly-laid concrete sidewalk, the RECOMMENDED procedure before finishing is to 21.____

    A. allow it to evaporate
    B. remove it with a broom
    C. sprinkle some dry cement on top
    D. remove it with a float

22. Terrazzo floors are laid with brass dividing strips PRIMARILY for the purpose of 22.____

    A. preventing slipping
    B. appearance
    C. preventing irregular cracking
    D. easy screeding

23. A #4 reinforcing bar has a diameter, in inches, of APPROXIMATELY 23.____

    A. 1/4   B. 3/8   C. 1/2   D. 5/8

24. The material that would NORMALLY be used to make a corbel in a brick wall is 24.____

    A. brick   B. wood   C. steel   D. concrete

25. A slab of concrete is 2'0" by 3'0" by 8" thick. The weight of the slab is, in pounds, MOST NEARLY 25.____

    A. 450   B. 500   C. 550   D. 600

KEY (CORRECT ANSWERS)

1. B	11. B
2. D	12. C
3. C	13. A
4. B	14. B
5. D	15. B
6. A	16. D
7. C	17. B
8. A	18. A
9. C	19. C
10. A	20. A

21. A
22. C
23. C
24. A
25. D

TEST 3

DIRECTIONS: Each question or incomplete statement is followed by several suggested answers or completions. Select the one that BEST answers the question or completes the statement. *PRINT THE LETTER OF THE CORRECT ANSWER IN THE SPACE AT THE RIGHT.*

1. Aggregates used to make concrete do NOT include

   A. sand
   B. gravel
   C. cement
   D. crushed rock

2. Careful slushing of the end joints of slip sills is PRIMARILY required to

   A. prevent displacement
   B. provide watertightness
   C. maintain bond
   D. prevent discoloration

3. Neat cement and marble chips are used

   A. as mortar in marble walls and floors
   B. to make terrazzo
   C. for stucco
   D. for ornamental ceilings

4. The tool shown at the right is a

   A. float
   B. finishing trowel
   C. hawk
   D. roofing seamer

5. A trimmer arch is used in connection with a

   A. fireplace
   B. window
   C. closet door
   D. stairway

6. A masonry nail is shown in sketch number

   A. 1
   B. 2
   C. 3
   D. 4

7. The coarse aggregate used in making terrazzo floors is MOST usually chips of

   A. limestone   B. granite   C. brick   D. marble

8. Reinforcing steel for a footing resting on earth can BEST be held at the specified distance above the earth by means of

   A. concrete blocks
   B. chairs
   C. bolsters
   D. hangers

9. A deformed reinforcing rod is superior to an equivalent smooth rod because it

   A. permits better bond with the concrete
   B. has greater tensile strength
   C. weighs more
   D. is easier to bend

10. Silt is harmful to the formation of strong concrete.
    Of the following ingredients of concrete, the one that is MOST likely to have the LARGEST amount of silt is

    A. cement
    B. fine aggregate
    C. coarse aggregate
    D. water

11. After a wedge-shaped hole has been cut into the large stone, the three-legged lifting device is inserted to lift the stone. The CORRECT order for inserting the three legs is

    A. 1, 2, 3
    B. 3, 2, 1
    C. 2, 3, 1
    D. 1, 3, 2

12. Specifications for a reinforced concrete structure call for a roof fill to be placed on the concrete roof slab.
    Of the following, the purpose of the fill is to

    A. reduce sound transmission
    B. facilitate drainage
    C. provide a smooth base for insulation
    D. protect the concrete slab

13. The code requires various thicknesses of concrete cover for reinforcing rods used in the different elements of a building.
    That element which requires the LEAST cover is

    A. column   B. beam   C. girder   D. flat slab

14. One cubic foot of dry sand weighs MOST NEARLY _____ lbs.

    A. 70   B. 94   C. 110   D. 150

15. The code provides that cold bends in reinforcing bars for concrete work shall have a radius at least equal to the least dimension of the bar multiplied by

    A. 1   B. 2   C. 3   D. 4

16. In acceptable concrete practice, a small w/c ratio is MOST likely to indicate that the concrete mix will

    A. be stiff
    B. produce high-strength concrete
    C. have a big slump
    D. produce low-strength concrete

17. In concrete work, wooden form spreaders should be removed

    A. as soon as the concrete is placed
    B. after the concrete has attained initial set
    C. after the concrete has attained final set
    D. after the concrete has attained full strength

18. A dove-tail anchor would MOST likely be used to bond brick veneer with a _____ wall.

    A. brick   B. concrete
    C. wood frame   D. concrete block

19. The use of bats in brick work is justified when such use

    A. is required by the bond
    B. reduces the amount of face brick
    C. eliminates headers
    D. prevents waste of excess bats

20. In an elevation view, round reinforcing bars in a reinforced concrete floor would appear as

    A. circles   B. lines
    C. either circles or lines   D. triangles

21. A groove is cut in the underside of a stone sill. This is done to

    A. keep rain water from running down the wall
    B. allow the insertion of dowels
    C. improve the mortar bond
    D. reduce the weight of the sill

22. An inspector picks up a brick, which has just been laid, to inspect the bedding. No mortar adhered to the brick so the furrowing of the mortar is shown clearly.
    The inspector is MOST concerned with the

    A. depth of the furrow
    B. width of the furrow
    C. depth and width of the furrow
    D. fact that no mortar adhered to the brick

23. It is necessary to burn reinforcing steel while they are in the wood forms in order to change their lengths.
The STANDARD safety precaution to observe during this process is to

    A. fireproof the wood forms
    B. use a low heat flame
    C. have a man stand by with a fire extinguisher
    D. soak a 20-foot radius around the area with water

24. When dowels are used in expansion joints, they are USUALLY

    A. covered with tar paper for about half the length to destroy the bond in one of the two adjacent slabs
    B. covered with tar paper over the entire length to destroy the bond in both slabs
    C. not covered so that the bond will be a maximum in both slabs
    D. covered with tar paper over the center portion only in order to protect it against rusting

25. Bricks are usually so placed in a brick wall that joints between bricks in any row do not line up with joints in the row immediately above and the one immediately below. The MAIN purpose of this staggering of bricks is to

    A. obtain a pleasing design
    B. make it easier to keep the successive rows level when laying the bricks
    C. prevent rain water from running in channels down the wall
    D. form a firmer wall

KEY (CORRECT ANSWERS)

1.	C	11.	D
2.	B	12.	B
3.	B	13.	D
4.	A	14.	C
5.	A	15.	B
6.	B	16.	B
7.	D	17.	A
8.	A	18.	B
9.	A	19.	A
10.	B	20.	C

21. A
22. D
23. C
24. A
25. D

WORK SCHEDULING
EXAMINATION SECTION
TEST 1

DIRECTIONS: Each question or incomplete statement is followed by several suggested answers or completions. Select the one that BEST answers the question or completes the statement. *PRINT THE LETTER OF THE CORRECT ANSWER IN THE SPACE AT THE RIGHT.*

Questions 1-8.

DIRECTIONS: Questions 1 through 8 are to be answered on the basis of the following information.

Assume that you are the supervisor of a unit that works seven days a week. You need to determine the work and vacation schedules of the employees you supervise for the month of July.

THE EMPLOYEES

Alan W.	9 years seniority	computer operator
Jane B.	4 1/2 years seniority	typist
Alex H.	5 years seniority	security staff
Tony E.	4 years seniority	security staff
Andre T.	4 2/3 years seniority	typist
Mary W.	11 years seniority	security staff
Andy R.	13 years seniority	computer operator
Rhonda L.	2 years seniority	computer operator
Ethel R.	15 years seniority	typist
Roger G.	3 years seniority	security staff

THE VACATION PREFERENCES OF THE EMPLOYEES:

	1st vacation day	1ast vacation day
Alan W.	7/1	7/19
Jane B.	7/15	7/29
Alex H.	7/8	7/22
Tony E.	7/22	7/30
Andre T.	7/1	7/14
Mary W.	7/1	7/22
Andy R.	7/15	7/30
Rhonda L.	7/20	7/31
Ethel R.	7/1	7/27
Roger G.	7/21	7/31

IMPORTANT REGULATIONS REGARDING VACATION LEAVE

Employees with seniority have first choice for their preferred vacation dates. Seniority should be calculated separately for each of the three occupational groups.

2 (#1)

There must be two security employees on duty each working day in July. This overrides any other considerations.

There must be one typist on duty each working day in July. This overrides any other considerations.

Employees with least seniority, when denied their first choice of vacation dates, should automatically be scheduled ahead for vacation on the very next date closest to the dates they had originally preferred and the length of the vacation extended the appropriate number of days. Example: A vacation originally requested for 7/13, but changed because of seniority, would be moved AHEAD to a date after 7/13 (to 7/16, for example).

You may want to use the calendar below to help you organize this information.
JULY

1	2	3	4	5	6	7
8	9	10	11	12	13	14
15	16	17	18	19	20	21
22	23	24	25	26	27	28
29	30	31				

1. The number of employees on vacation on July 16 should be
   A. four   B. five   C. six   D. seven

2. The number of employees on vacation on July 22 should be
   A. five   B. six   C. seven   D. eight

3. How many typists will be working on July 15?
   A. One   B. Two   C. Three   D. None

4. How many workers will be on vacation on July 31?
   A. Two   B. Three   C. Four   D. Five

5. Which of the following is TRUE of the employees in the unit?
   I. Andy R., Jane B., Tony E., and Mary W. will be on vacation on 7/22.
   II. Ethel R., Andre T., Mary W., and Alex H. will be on vacation on 7/8.

III. Rhonda L., Tony E., and Roger G. will be on vacation on 7/31,
IV. Andy R., Jane B., and Ethel R. will be on vacation on 7/28.
THE CORRECT ANSWER IS:

A. I, II, III B. I, II
C. II, III D. II

5._____

6. How many typists will be working on July 28?

A. One B. Two C. Three D. Four

6._____

7. How many computer operators will be working on July 23?

A. One B. Two C. Three D. Four

7._____

8. Roger G. will begin his vacation on July

A. 21 B. 22 C. 23 D. 24

8._____

Questions 9-15.

DIRECTIONS: Questions 9 through 15 are to be answered on the basis of the following information.

Assume that you are the supervisor of a unit that works seven days a week. You need to determine the work and vacation schedules of the employees you supervise for the month of August.

THE EMPLOYEES

	Years Seniority	Position
Robert L.	7	Security staff
Ann N.	7 1/2	Computer operator
Thomas B.	9	Typist
Phyllis P.	11	Computer operator
Mike D.	3	Security staff
Jane R.	2	Security staff
Alan R.	8	Computer operator
Susan T.	10	Typist
George W.	6	Computer operator
Barbara L.	4	Typist
Jack B.	13	Security staff
Grace N.	12	Typist

THE VACATION PREFERENCES OF THE EMPLOYEES

	1st vacation day	last vacation day
Robert L.	8/3	8/18
Ann N.	8/17	8/28
Thomas B.	8/19	8/28
Phyllis P.	8/5	8/20
Mike D.	8/14	8/21
Jane R.	8/20	8/27
Alan R.	8/12	8/26
Susan T.	8/5	8/26
George W.	8/3	8/14
Barbara L.	8/7	8/21
Jack B.	8/10	8/18
Grace N.	8/4	8/25

4 (#1)

IMPORTANT REGULATIONS REGARDING VACATION LEAVE.

Employees with seniority have first choice for their preferred vacation dates. Seniority should be calculated separately for each of the three occupational groups.

There must be two security employees on duty each working day in August. This overrides any other considerations.

There must be two typists on duty from 8/11 to 8/18. This overrides any other considerations.

There must be two computer operators on duty each working day in August. This overrides any other considerations.

Employees with least seniority, when denied their first choice of vacation dates, should automatically be scheduled ahead for their vacation on the very next date closest to the date they originally preferred, and the length of the vacation extended the appropriate number of days. Example: A vacation originally requested for 8/18, but changed because of seniority, would be moved AHEAD to a date after 8/18 (to 8/21, for example).

You may wish to use the calendar on the next page to help you organize this information.

AUGUST

1	2	3	4	5	6	7
8	9	10	11	12	13	14
15	16	17	18	19	20	21
22	23	24	25	26	27	28
29	30	31				

9. How many workers will be on vacation on August 21?　　　　　　　　　　　　　　　　9.____
　　A. Five　　　　　B. Six　　　　　C. Seven　　　　　D. Eight

10. How many workers will be working on August 28?　　　　　　　　　　　　　　　　10.____
　　A. Six　　　　　B. Seven　　　　　C. Eight　　　　　D. Nine

11. Of the following, who will NOT work on August 27?   11._____
    A. Alan R.   B. George W.   C. Mike D.   D. Susan T.

12. Of the following, who will work on August 19?   12._____
    A. Thomas B.   B. Barbara L.
    C. Ann N.   D. Mike D.

13. How many typists will be on vacation on August 19?   13._____
    A. One   B. Two   C. Three   D. Four

14. How many workers will be on vacation on August 17?   14._____
    A. Five   B. Six   C. Eight   D. Nine

15. How many workers will work on August 11?   15._____
    A. Seven   B. Eight   C. Five   D. Six

KEY (CORRECT ANSWERS)

1.	C	6.	B	11.	B
2.	B	7.	A	12.	C
3.	A	8.	C	13.	D
4.	B	9.	D	14.	B
5.	C	10.	C	15.	A

www.ingramcontent.com/pod-product-compliance
Lightning Source LLC
Chambersburg PA
CBHW080740230426
43665CB00020B/2803